Blue Star

Fulfilling Prophecy

by
Miriam Delicado

Cover art by Corey Wolfe

Edited by Leah Gough

Edited by Leah Gough

Cover art by Corey Wolfe
www.coreywolfe.com

Author contact:
www.alienbluestar.com

Order this book online at www.trafford.com
or email orders@trafford.com

Most Trafford titles are also available at major online book retailers.

Print information available on the last page.

ISBN: 978-1-4251-3207-1 (sc)
ISBN: 978-1-4251-5400-4 (hc)
ISBN: 978-1-4251-3209-5 (e)

Because of the dynamic nature of the Internet, any web addresses or links contained in this book may have changed since publication and may no longer be valid. The views expressed in this work are solely those of the author and do not necessarily reflect the views of the publisher, and the publisher hereby disclaims any responsibility for them.

Any people depicted in stock imagery provided by Thinkstock are models, and such images are being used for illustrative purposes only. Certain stock imagery © Thinkstock.

Trafford rev. 04/08/2015

 www.trafford.com

North America & international
toll-free: 1 888 232 4444 (USA & Canada)
fax: 812 355 4082

Acknowledgements

This book is dedicated to all the people, too many to name, who have shown their support to me over the years; you know who you are. I thank you for your unconditional acceptance and encouragement.

I would like to say a special thank you to Rhonda and Kathleen who were there from the beginning of this adventure. Your acceptance of me helped keep me grounded and held me together when I felt like I was falling apart.

To Rick, Marcella, Jane, Karla, and Corey, who always encouraged me to do whatever it took to get my story to the public, I thank you for your steadfast belief in me.

A special thank you to my sister Juliana who always encouraged me to pursue my intuitive gifts and be proud of them.

Finally, I dedicate this book to you, the reader, as every word was written with you in mind. May my story help you along your path to finding the truth of who we are and what role each of us has to play on the planet today.

"*I believe the quality of relationship you have with yourself and the people around you affects the Earth more than we choose to recognize. If we choose to learn to communicate consciously with compassion we would change the world we live in.*"

Karla Dombroski

CONTENTS

YOU CAN REACH THE AUTHOR THROUGH HER WEB SITE AT:

www.alienbluestar.com

Introduction

After an abduction experience in 1988, everything in my world changed forever. In *Blue Star* I share with you the events that took place after my encounter with the Tall Blond Aliens. I attempt to show you how and why I have come to the conclusions I have regarding this contact.

This was not an easy book to write because of the complexity of the story itself. Having no formal education past the eighth grade, I found writing this book was a challenge. Yet, as I began the process of writing I knew that if I followed my instinct to share my life story as if you were a friend, it would become a complete story. Under the guidance of the Aliens, I found I was able to write an entire book, despite my lack of formal education.

I chose to share with you the chronological order in which the facts were presented to me. For this reason you may be asking yourself questions as you begin to read this book, just as I asked myself the same questions. As my story unfolds you will find answers to those questions, demonstrating how all the facts fit together.

One of my main concerns regarding sharing my story has been to protect my family and friends from any unwanted attention. For this reason, I have chosen to change the names of the characters involved with the exception of my own. Furthermore, although the town in which I grew up was in Northern British Columbia, I chose the setting of Cranbrook for my book—again to protect the people involved. The real locations of all other events are the true locations. Every piece of information I share in this book comes from my *direct* knowledge from the Aliens or from my actual experience. Every word of this book represents the true events of my life. There is no part of this story that is fictional in any way.

In sharing this story I am fulfilling a direct request by the Aliens. My goal and the goal of the Aliens is to open your mind to the truth: we are not alone, they are watching and there is no reason to fear them.

Thank you,

Miriam Delicado

OH GREAT SPIRIT

Oh Great Spirit that lay within
I can hear your heart like the ocean and wind
Gentle like raindrops powerful as stars
I can feel your beat as it travels far

Oh Great Spirit that lay within
Teach me the world as it slowly spins
Show me a rainbow from Heaven to Earth
Teach me to travel without leaving my perch

Oh Great Spirit that lay within
I'll follow your voice if I hear you sing
Loud and clear the song must be
Help me to follow the Great Symphony

Oh Great Spirit that lay within
My heart is as strong as a sacred wind
It dances with nature calls to the wild
Plays with the children and tames the Great Fire

Oh Great Spirit that lay within
I've learned the knowledge that comes from within
My Spirit it soars with Massauu it sings
Travels on rainbows as the next stage begins

THE BEGINNING

The date was March 10ᵗʰ, 1966 when I made my way into this world. At the time of my birth I had two sisters: Janice who was four-years old and Carol who was two. After leaving the hospital I was taken to the home I was to live in for the next nine years. It was a tiny two-bedroom place, so small that the kitchen, living room and dining area were all in one. It was more like a bachelor suite than a family home; yet everything seems bigger when you are a child.

When I was a baby I remember lying in my crib, unable to move very well. I remember looking at my mother and crying, trying very hard to talk to her, but the sounds I wanted wouldn't come out of my mouth. I could sometimes understand what my parents were talking about but there was no way I could communicate with them. When I was much older I told both my parents some of the conversations I remembered them having. They were shocked I remembered because I was only a baby at the time!

When I graduated from my crib to a bed I moved into my sisters' room. It was tiny and only had enough room for two single beds. I had to share a bed with one of my sisters. Usually I slept with Janice, holding onto her as I fell asleep. I wanted to hold on so that if I was taken from my bed I would know because I wouldn't be able to feel her there anymore. Where I was to be taken, I never knew. It was a powerful feeling that was always in my mind as I fell asleep.

My sisters and I didn't have many toys growing up: only one full box and that was it. The three of us had to share all our toys, clothes and beds; nothing belonged to just one of us. A lot of our time was spent playing outside in the farmers' fields, in the bushes that lined the river, on the dry riverbed or climbing trees. We didn't have much so we made our own fun playing with the other kids in the area.

The feeling I was somehow different from other people began when I was a young child and continued throughout my life. I would often look at people as they passed on the street and wonder about their thoughts. My favourite game was to look at a person and try to figure out what they were thinking. Sometimes what popped into my head was not always positive and when that happened I would stop trying to see anything else from that person and move on to the next. I feared that I would get in trouble for hearing what they were thinking, but I did it anyway.

I gave a lot of thought to my parents from the time I was very young. I couldn't help but think that somehow I was with the wrong family and that one day when I got older I would discover the truth: these people were not related to me. I never felt fully connected to them.

When we were young my father would take us for walks and show us the different plants in the area around our home explaining what was edible and what wasn't. He talked a lot about how we could survive living off the land. One of my few fond memories of my father was of him carving us flutes out of tree brush as we walked along the river that ran past our home.

My father was a controlling man, coming from a strong European background. His idea of family was to raise us with a strong disciplinary hand. This made our family life difficult and made all of us unhappy.

My father was a man that stood out from the crowd no matter where he was or what he was doing. When I was a young child growing up in our small town, it seemed like everyone knew him. They gave him terrible nicknames and my sisters and I would be heckled during school breaks—often brutally hit and pushed as they hollered insults at us about our father.

They heckled us because of his teaching of herbal remedies and holistic approach to health and living. The stories he told us as children were often geared towards how to take care of ourselves in the event that the world as we knew it ever came to an end. Survival skills were a constant focus; he told us that one day when everyone else was starving we would be able to eat because we knew what plants in the area were edible. He had us pick herbs that he would then dry out to make tea for different ailments. At the time it was embarrassing and not the normal type of upbringing.

My father taught us how to build survival shelters in summer as well as winter. He would quiz us on how to do these things if we ever needed to.

His knowledge seemed to be endless and it often made no sense to me why he was so determined to teach us all of these strange things. Most times his ramblings were geared towards things I was too young to comprehend. Yet I was forced to listen and learn.

He used to point at the mountains surrounding our town of Cranbrook, explaining that if there was nuclear war in the future it would be one of the safest places to be. He told us that if nuclear war ever happened on the other side of the world the poison in the clouds would follow the Earth's air currents. The nuclear clouds would then have to drop most of their radiation before they could lift high enough to get over the mountains and rain on us. He told my sisters and I this story many times. I didn't know why he thought this and there was no way to know if his strange ideas were true or not. I didn't understand how any of it had to do with me. I wondered what air currents were and how he knew they would protect us. Instead of telling less of these strange stories, as I got older he began to tell us even more.

My mother was a highly intelligent woman who went back to work shortly after I turned three. Life was not easy for her with my father constantly yelling and berating her. She was forced to listen to his rambling stories also, but never wanted to hear them. My mom was a strong woman and everyone who knew her had a great deal of respect for her. She worked a lot but she always seemed to find the time to bake for us. I have wonderful memories of her making us baked goodies: bread, cakes, doughnuts and my favourite, cinnamon rolls.

In our small community my father was infamous and most people thought he was delusional. He often told people how he was superior because of his genes. As children we were told that we too had these "special, superior" genes. I never understood what he was talking about or why he would say such a thing. It sounded crazy to my sisters and I. He told me specifically that because I was *his* daughter I was somehow superior and special. I never understood what he meant by the statement or why he told us the things he did.

When we were children we would have to sit quietly as my father talked to his friends for hours about his life. He was very young when he began to fight in the army during the Second World War. He said that he fought for more than one country: France, Italy and Yugoslavia. How this came about I never knew but it seemed to have ripped his soul in pieces. It most assuredly changed him in a negative way: when he spoke of the war it was often with a great deal of anger and resentment.

My father often told a story about being on the streets of Paris during the war when a man approached him. This man asked him to go and work for what my father called "The Russian Psychic Army." He used to say, "Never ever go with them! What do they think I'm stupid? You work for them and you can never leave, they will kill you, they own you. You can't hide! There is nowhere to hide on this planet; they are some of the strongest psychics in the world and they can find you with their minds. They don't need to use a gun to kill you—they do it with their minds. Don't ever go with them, do you understand?" Of course when he told me this story I told him I understood even though I didn't, not at that time. My sisters had the same lecture regarding these "men" on many occasions. We knew that our father was psychic because he knew things sometimes that proved to us he had the ability to see the future. He always knew when the phone would ring and who it was before we told him. He told us all the time that he had psychic ability. As we grew older we saw him do little things all the time that proved to us he actually was psychic.

As we were growing up, my mother was often busy at work while trying to keep up with the piles of laundry that always seemed to fill our tiny home. By the time I went to grade one, my father had changed careers due to an accident as a logger. He began working as a bricklayer. This new career led him and my mother to decided to build a house. For Janice, Carol and I this meant that for the next three years after school we had to go help my dad and his friends with this project. We were small helpers but we worked hard. When it got dark the lights of the truck lit our way so we could lay a few more bricks before going home.

We often ate our supper at the building site and we sometimes put apples on top of the wood-burning barrel to cook. We kept warm at the fire while the ordinary apples changed to a sweet treat—always a highlight of our time at the location of our new home.

In 1976 we finally moved to our new four-bedroom, spacious, two-level home. There was still a lot of work to be done but I felt like we were moving into a mansion. At first I had to share a room with my sister, Carol, because we only had two beds. It didn't take long before I got my own room. After sharing a bed with one of my sisters all my life it was strange to have my own room—let alone my own bed.

Almost from the beginning, my family felt there was a presence in the house with us. None of us knew what or who it may be. My sisters and I never wanted to go into the basement alone because we could feel the presence of something down there. We often talked about the feeling we all had and wondered if maybe we had built our home on an ancient burial ground that we were not aware of.

Over the next few years almost everyone who came into our home would have some kind of paranormal experience with this entity. Often my entire family would be kept awake all night by the stomping and dragging sounds in the house and on the stairs. It was awful and it bothered everyone in our home.

There were times when the entity would be exceptionally bad. In one such case a friend of my father was staying with us, using the bedroom in the basement. Apparently he was lying on the bed when, all of a sudden, a small ball that was in the room began to jump. It was moving so fast and hard that it hit the ceiling and bounced from the floor to the ceiling over and over. Nothing in the room was moving except the ball and he never touched it.

I wasn't home when this happened but heard about it from my family. They said he ran up the stairs, scared to death. He then left the house and told us he wouldn't return to pick up his belongings. We had to pack them up for him because he refused to come anywhere near our home again.

The entity would often keep members of my family awake all night with its noise. Sometimes it would go on for days on end with no relief. The strange thing was, I never saw or heard anything although I could always feel the negative energy in the basement. It was as though it knew better than to mess with me. Often it would act up the strongest when I was not around and I would hear about its antics later.

This was when my psychic ability began to awaken. Sometimes I would lie in bed at night and have a conversation with this negative energy. When it would act up for long periods of time and keep my family from sleeping, I would do a small ritual to protect us from it.

"Dear God," I would say. "Please protect me and my family from whoever or whatever lives in the basement. By Universal Law you are not allowed to bother anyone who is of less power than you. So if you go to anyone tonight you have to go through me. Amen."

The next day I would ask my family how they slept. Happily, they would report they slept though the night for the first time in days or, sometimes, weeks. They normally reported that they did not hear or see anything all night. I never told them about my protection prayer.

Whenever I woke from a night after this prayer I would have memories of standing in our basement with red flames across the room that engulfed the other half of the basement. I would stand with my eyes fixed on the flames, repeating a prayer over and over again, not allowing the energy/entity to pass me. Sometimes I kept up this ritual for days at a time even though it took a lot out of me.

The entity in the basement stayed with our home until I was much older—23-years old—at which time I did a ritual to have it move on. Again, I did not tell my family what I had done. When I asked Janice if the energy was still around, she happily reported that it seemed to have left and was no longer a bother to anyone. It was only after she told me it left that I informed her of all I had done for our family and our home.

The older I got, the more these abilities began to surface. Often I didn't fully understand how they worked—just that they did. When I was in grade five my friend Trish and I were sitting in the gymnasium for a school assembly. As usual we were talking and not paying attention. She was showing me her hands and telling me how embarrassed she was by them. I couldn't blame her: they did look ugly. Small warts covered both her hands from her fingertips to wrists.

Trish told me how she had tried everything to get rid of them but nothing worked. I then told her not to worry I would take them away for her. Of course, she wondered what I was talking about. I told her, "All I have to do is hold your hands for a minute and they will go away." She was doubtful that it would work but I talked her into letting me try.

There I was, in the middle of assembly, holding Trish's hands. I closed my eyes and pictured the warts dissolving and her hands turning smooth and clear. A minute later I opened my eyes and chuckled. Trish asked me what I had done because she could feel her hands tingle while I held them. With a smile on my face I told her the warts would be gone in about a week. I knew she didn't believe me but I also knew that in a couple of weeks she would be shocked.

Within two weeks Trish saw me in the hallway at school and excitedly showed me her hands. They were no longer covered in warts. The doctor told her that they sometimes suddenly disappear—she didn't want to believe it was my hands that had taken her warts away. *I knew* that it was my energy that had healed her! I didn't push it, if someone doesn't want to believe in the supernatural, they won't—no matter what you do or say.

By the time I was 12-years old the situation with my father's strong hand was no longer acceptable and I left home to live in foster care. The next few years I bounced from foster homes to group homes, sometimes running away to stay with friends. This was a very difficult time in my life.

The following year was like a whirlwind of disaster after disaster for me. Drugs and alcohol became part of my way of coping with the stress of my family life. Thankfully this phase only lasted about one year. It didn't take me long to realize that it was not the way I wanted to live my life.

When I was 13-years old I had very few friends. Due to my family life and my strange abilities I wasn't comfortable with many people. I did, however, share my special gifts with two of my friends, Darlene and Nicole. On one particular night Darlene and I were very worried about Nicole. No one had seen her for a couple of days and Darlene asked me if I could use my special ability to find her.

Unsure how or if my gift would work I reluctantly decided to try. I laid down on Darlene's bed and tried to concentrate on Nicole's face. At first I saw only darkness. In the next moment I clearly saw an old blue car traveling on the highway towards the next town over. I knew this because I saw a sign on the side of the road. It was as though I was sitting in the back seat of the car as a passenger. I could see Nicole in the front passenger seat laughing while an older man—whom I did not recognize—drove.

When I opened my eyes I told Darlene everything I saw, including a description of the man. She didn't know who he was either, and at that point she asked me if Nicole was okay with him. I reassured her that she was alright and would be back safely in a couple of days. I knew this because while I observed them they talked about how long they would be gone.

We waited to hear from Nicole—not only to see if she was okay but we both wanted to know if my vision was correct or not. Three days later, at school, we saw Nicole walking down the hall towards us. She was smiling as she said hello. Without hesitation Darlene began to ask the many questions we wanted answers to. Where was she the past few days, who was she with and why didn't she let us know she was okay?

Nicole was not amused by our interrogation. She did, however, confirm that she was in Kimberly, the next town over, with a man that drove a blue car. We then told Nicole why we were asking all the questions. The three of us were taken aback by the accuracy of the whole incident and agreed that it was really strange that I had seen everything with such clarity.

Over the next year many more incidents happened which were just as detailed and accurate as the night with Nicole. Sometimes I would tell people my visions and sometimes I wouldn't. Sometimes I would try to see into the future, other times I would have dreams or visions that would simply pop into my mind. No matter how the information came, I found it to be accurate.

As 1979 came to an end I no longer thought I was different—I knew I was. My gifts were becoming as natural as breathing; I began to feel that if I didn't have the gift of sight I wouldn't feel whole. In some ways it was a curse to see events like a death or an accident, especially when it involved a friend. Although I didn't realize it at the time, it was through all of these experiences I was learning about my gifts as well as who I was.

In 1980, at the age of fourteen, I was living at home for the first time in almost two years. Two months after I got there my father decided to go on one of his rampages. I quickly chose to leave rather than fight with him and I went for a long walk in the rain. It was dark and the trees no longer had their leaves. I remember thinking how dismal it all seemed, the heavy downpour soaking me as I walked the streets alone.

Something inside me made me stop on the sidewalk and look straight up. As I did I gave thanks for my life and all I had in it. *One day I will help many people, that is what I am here for and all this will be worth it in the end.* Why I was thinking this wasn't clear but it was a strong and impressive moment in my life. Hours later, cold and tired, I made my way back home.

I quickly realized that it was no longer bearable for me to live with my parents and I made the decision to leave permanently. There was no life for me within the walls of my father's home. It was a decision that changed everything—then and well into my future.

Sadly, there were very few options left open for me. Being only fourteen-years old it was difficult for me to find work. My father had created problems for himself as well as me with the people at Social Services and they, in turn, decided not to give me a place to live. They were afraid of him and, since he wanted me home, they wouldn't place me in protective care.

The next few decisions I made were based on survival. There was no way I could convince Social Services to give me a foster home to live in; my options were limited. Even though I was young I understood that if I went back home to my father one of us would not survive. My mind was strong and clear that I would no longer allow him to mistreat me.

It was only three days after my fourteenth birthday when it became official that I was completely on my own. The decision to move in with my boyfriend, Darren, was an easy one. He was six years older than me so I knew he would be able to take care of me. I knew living with him was my way out of the hell I lived in with my father.

My education was no longer an option since the school I was attending told me that if I was not at home or in a group home I couldn't attend school. I was hurt and sad that I wouldn't be allowed to attend college either because of my age. The reality of my situation was undeniable and I knew the decision I made to leave home would be throwing me into a difficult life: no education equals no good jobs and no money. I made the decision with my eyes wide open.

Over the next four years Darren and I lived together. I shared with him my psychic ability but he wasn't interested in talking about it with me. Sometimes I would pass my hand over Darren's back as though I was touching him. Unknown to him I would have my hand at least two inches from his skin. It would tickle him as my hand scanned above his body even though I was not actually touching him physically. I knew that if he ever found out what I was doing he wouldn't want me to do it anymore. I practiced using my energy on him to help me gain control over it.

My visions and dreams didn't end during this time. There were many psychic incidents that took place over the years and I often shared them with my older sister, Janice. She couldn't give me any advice on them but she was always supportive of my gift.

One day I woke from a deep sleep very upset. I had had an extremely clear vision of an airplane crash. It was awful! I could see the people in their seats, the plane taking off, the sky, the runway and many other details. I saw the crash and hundreds of people dead. I shared this vision with Janice. She asked me what airline it was but I couldn't see the name. She encouraged me to look at the vision again to find more details to the event. Unfortunately I couldn't see anything more. I was helpless to the vision and didn't understand why I was shown the accident if I couldn't change it.

Three days later, the news reported a plane crash with over two hundred people. It went down with no survivors. I was upset for a long time over the disturbing news. I never understood what the purpose of the vision served.

There have been many incidents over the years in which I had been given such detailed sight that I sometimes had a difficult time knowing what to do with the information. I was still only learning about my gift. The knowledge that came to me was like going to school. Slowly, step by step I came to accept that I was different from most people I knew. Each vision gave me clearer insight into myself as well as my gift.

Once I had a vision of my sister, Carol, driving down a street that was on a hill. It was winter and I could see that she hit black ice, spun out of control and went over the embankment. I warned her of the vision and as a result she drove very slowly on the hill on her way home from school that day. She did skid on a patch of black ice but because she was traveling so slowly she didn't go over the embankment and kept the car under control.

Another time, my friend, Nicole, introduced me to her new boyfriend. The next day I saw him clearly on the side of the highway, his car stopped. I then saw him with blood on his face. He was thrown from the car and was pulling himself onto the road from the ditch. There were no other cars involved in the accident. In this case I couldn't track him or Nicole down to tell them my vision. What was the point of me seeing this if I couldn't help? I found out the following day that the event did in fact take place and he was not seriously injured.

My relationship with Darren finally came to an end after four years when I was getting close to legal age. In the past year I had taken on three jobs and was making very good wages for myself. Since the arrangement with Darren was made under extraordinary circumstances, I was more than ready to leave the situation.

The adjustment to single life was exhilarating. I lived on my own for a short time and then found a roommate. Her name was Sally. We were the same age and she too came from a difficult family life. A mutual friend introduced us and it didn't take long for us to become the best of friends. We lived together for just under a year before she moved to Vancouver with her boyfriend, Stewart.

Shortly after my nineteenth birthday I started to go out with my friends. I had a lot of fun after years of being isolated. I felt like a whole new person. It was my first taste of being really alive—free from family and Darren.

Over the next few months several incidents happened that again would bring my gifts to the surface. Around this time Janice began living with me as the situation at home became unbearable for her. A couple of weeks later she attended a friend's wedding. After the reception was over she asked two of the relatives of the bride if they wanted to come by our home to have a few more drinks.

I wasn't very happy to see my sister so late with two total strangers in my house, but I didn't want to be rude to the brothers. Over the next few hours Janice sat on one couch with one of the brothers while I sat on the other couch with the other. We each had separate conversations for hours until we all began talking and, to our surprise, we were all talking about the same thing: me! I told the brothers that I had psychic ability. After some taunting by the three of them I began to read one of the brothers. Before beginning I asked him if it was what he wanted and if he would let me see into his life with my gift of ESP. After he agreed I began to give him intimate details of his life. I explained the home he lived in and described the room in which he spent most of his time with incredible detail. I did this by looking into his eyes—nothing more.

I was so accurate in even the smallest details that he tried to throw me off by telling me that I was completely wrong. Even after he said this I continued telling him details of his most private life. After a couple more minutes he jumped up and said he was leaving and told me to stop. He was yelling at his brother to come with him immediately. It was obvious to me that I was accurate and I was scaring him. It was not my intention to frighten him, but there was nothing I could say to calm him at that point.

The following day Janice went to her friend's home for a small gathering of guests and family from the wedding the day prior. There, the brother I read the night before told her that I had scared him badly. He told her that I was so accurate that he tried to throw me off by telling me I was wrong. When I continued to tell him things that I couldn't possibly have known with such detail, he became terrified and had to leave. Janice assured him that I wasn't still looking at his life the way I had the night before.

It was obvious that I had a natural gift of sight. My reading of the brother was the first time I was so detailed and accurate while making a conscious effort to use my psychic ability. In some ways it scared me as well because at that point I wasn't fully in control of it. For some reason I couldn't shut it off once it began, and for days I couldn't look anyone in the eye or I would get flashes of their private lives. It was a difficult few days.

Not being familiar with this new opened doorway I went to my friend Anna, the only person I thought that may have some insight into what was happening to me. When I went to her home I explained the past two days' events and asked her to help me close the doorway I had opened. She went to her kitchen cupboard and pulled out a deck of cards and began to test me by holding up a card and asking me what it was. After about eight cards I had every one of them wrong. Then all of a sudden Anna looked up at me, shocked. "Miriam, you're not guessing the card in my hand, you're telling me the card on the top of the deck! You didn't get any of them wrong—you got every one of them right!" When Anna said that my heart skipped a beat because I realized she was right!

After talking with her for a couple of hours she told me everything she could about what was happening to me. Even with her limited knowledge at the time, it was enough for me to shut the open doorway. I was relieved to be able to look at people again without receiving all of the flashing images of their personal and very private lives.

A couple of months after this major psychic experience, life in Cranbrook took on new challenges. Troubles at my parents' home made my life change once again and my second sister, Carol, came to stay with me. With both of my sisters in my home I was beginning to feel pressured. With everything that was going on around me I made the decision to go and visit a friend in Vancouver.

On September 3rd, 1985 I left Cranbrook with one borrowed suitcase and a new focus: to begin living my life for myself and not for anyone else. I arrived in the big city scared and in awe. On my first day in Vancouver I went out of my friend's apartment to go for a walk and got lost. I was terrified as I walked by all the people and buildings in this strange new place. The feelings that overwhelmed me gave me a strange sense of empowerment. It was a newfound freedom I had never experienced before and I liked it!

Three days after arriving in the big city I called my sisters. I told them that I wasn't coming back and they could keep my apartment if they wanted. As for all my things, they could sell or keep them—I didn't want anything from the life I left behind. Over the next three years I lived in the Vancouver area, moving often and trying to find my place in the world. It was strangely liberating to be so isolated from the familiar. Somehow being surrounded by strangers gives a person the courage to be who they are on the inside, so people can see who you really are on the outside.

THE HIGHWAY
(1988)

The year was 1988 and I was 22-years old. I left my hometown of Cranbrook at the age of 19 and had been living in Vancouver ever since. I was still relatively new to the city and was not unlike other 22-year olds—I went out often, taking in Vancouver's nightlife. When I first arrived I only knew two people that lived in the city. That changed as over the years a few more of my friends made the move. I was living with my boyfriend and, although things were not going as well as I would have liked, something kept me from leaving. Despite this feeling, I was having a great time exploring my new home and also getting to know who I was…or so I thought.

One early fall day I was home alone. I laid on the couch to take a nap and immediately felt myself traveling through a tunnel. It was as though I was being pulled along. I was looking at the stars all around me except there were three times as many as I would see in the sky at night. When I looked ahead of me I seemed to be traveling through a tunnel at tremendous speed. For never having seen anything like this before I was rather calm and intrigued by the whole process.

At the end of the tunnel I stopped and then I sat to talk with a man and woman. They both wore long white robes that covered their feet. The woman was beautiful. Her skin was like a china doll's and she had long blond hair. The man had dark hair that fell to just above his shoulders. They both had captivating blue eyes. It felt like we were sitting in the middle of the universe, there appeared to be stars all around us. It felt real to me when I was with them—nothing like a dream.

I woke 20 minutes later from this strange conversation, sat up and almost robotically began to pack my things to leave. I called my friend Sally and asked if I could stay with her and her boyfriend. Almost immediately, she and Stewart arrived to help move me into their home. Despite my quick departure, I couldn't seem to shake the encounter with the two beings in the tunnel. I didn't understand what had happened earlier that day and kept going over it in my mind. I had the feeling our meeting was of deep importance to me, but I couldn't remember what the man and woman had said.

After being at Sally's for about a week she asked me if I wanted to go to Cranbrook with her and her boyfriend. We would drive there and back so it wouldn't cost much for the three of us to visit our friends and family. Since I wasn't working I said I would go with them. We'd done this trip a number of times in the past so we knew it would take about thirteen hours. The only downfall was that Stewart would have to do all of the driving since Sally and I did not have our driver's licences.

We left Vancouver the following week. As usual just past Osoyoos, Stewart was too tired to keep driving so we pulled over for about three hours while he slept. Thirteen hours after leaving Vancouver we arrived safe and sound in Cranbrook. Sally and Stewart dropped me off at a friend's house and said they would contact me to let me know when we would be leaving. I spent the week visiting my friends and family.

I thought my friend Anna might have some explanation to the two beings I met in the tunnel. She was very spiritual and sometimes had explanations for things I didn't understand. Why did I see these beings to begin with? Did they want me to leave my boyfriend for some reason? After all, the way I left him was rather odd because it was so sudden. Maybe they knew something I didn't and were looking out for me. That was Anna's explanation. Maybe they were what she called my "spirit guides." That seemed like a reasonable explanation since I had always believed people were being watched over by angels.

The week flew by and Friday night rolled around rather quickly. It was my last night in town and I was out to have a good time before going back to Vancouver. I wanted to get drunk and party with friends. That decision led me to a miserable Saturday morning.

Feeling sick and tired I heaved my weary body back into the car that morning and prepared for the long drive back to Vancouver. Sally's sister, Heather, and her son who was 4-years old decided to come with us. That meant that we would have an extra driver so it would not take as long as usual to get home.

The journey back to Vancouver began uneventfully and was rather boring. I was happy to sit in the back seat and sleep since I was still nursing the consequences of the night before. We made the usual stops for gas, coffee and food. None of us wanted the trip to be longer than it had to be so the stops were brief. If possible we would take our purchases of food with us rather than sit around wasting time eating.

After dinner Heather's son was fast asleep between us in the back seat. The day faded into night and I was finally beginning to feel like myself. The hum of the engine kept me drifting in and out of sleep. As night crept in those beautiful stars that always seemed to elude us in the city began to show themselves. I was drifting off to sleep when boom!—just like I had weeks before I found myself being pulled through a tunnel. At the end I sat and spoke with the same man and woman as last time. When I woke I felt shaken, not only by the experience but by what I remembered them saying. They said to me, "Do not be afraid. We are your friends, we are your family. You have chosen to be here at this time. We are coming for you soon. Do not be afraid."

When I woke from this strange clear dream I was taken aback by it. I began to think about the last time I saw them in my dream on the couch and wondered what they meant by all they said to me. I wanted to tell Sally but what would I tell her? I stared out the window intently after the dream looking at the stars. I kept hearing the words play over and over in my mind, *We are coming for you soon*. How, why and when they were coming—none of what they said made any sense to me.

Stewart was driving and talking with Sally who was in the passenger seat. After a short time he asked Heather to take over driving so he could get some rest. That meant that I would now be the co-pilot as I moved into the front passenger seat to keep Heather company.

Since we had no tape player in the car we listened to the radio. Its signal would fade in and out so we left it on low volume, turning it down when we lost the signal and up when the music came on. We drove for a short time, talking. As always I stared at those beautiful stars.

There were fewer and fewer cars on the road as we drove through the night and it became darker and more solitary. We began driving on an incline that had a passing lane. It was at this moment that everything changed.

Both Heather and I noticed lights behind us that were closing the gap between the two cars rather quickly. I commented that they would pass us for sure because they were traveling so fast. The lights were odd: big and round, similar to those of a container truck but so bright that we couldn't see the vehicle at all. They didn't pass us. They stayed right on our tail all the way up the incline. Car lights crested the hill from the opposite direction; in that moment the lights behind us drifted back into the darkness and were gone.

For the next couple of hours these lights appeared and disappeared often. Each time they appeared a strange radio station could be heard, apparently broadcasting from somewhere in the Southwestern United States. This was more than a little weird and Heather and I talked about it. Each time the lights appeared they would catch-up to us very quickly but never pass. If there was a car coming towards us or if we went through a small town the lights would simply disappear, only to reappear in the blink of an eye. We were getting scared and questioned why they were following us so closely but never passing.

Heather and I were completely freaked out by the whole thing. The lights had come up behind us again and again and we wondered why they would never pass or stay behind us if anyone else was around. I knew the highway went straight through the next town we were coming to. It was a long distance from one end of the town to the other. I told Heather to drive as fast as she could so we could get as far as possible from the strange lights. As we turned the corner out of town they were nowhere to be seen. "Okay," I said. "There is no way they can catch us now!" No car driving the length of the highway through that town could have caught up to us. How wrong I was!

The minute we were out of sight of the town, poof, the lights reappeared. Neither Heather nor myself noticed them approaching—they were just suddenly there. " Where did they come from?" we screamed.

"There was no way they could have caught up with us!" I yelled. Again the strange radio station came on and we panicked. Heather yelled at me to watch them and poof! they were gone. I looked in the side mirror of the car and blinked. There they were again! I turned around to watch them and told Heather I wouldn't take my eyes off of them. Then I blinked and they were gone! Behind us was only darkness. "I didn't see them disappear!" I screamed.

"Do you see them Miriam?" Heather asked.

"No!" I yelled.

We both watched for them so we could see where they were coming from and where they went.

Finally Heather said, "Maybe it is a UFO!" I was very scared now!

The lights continued to appear and disappear more quickly. They no longer pulled back into the darkness. Instead it was like a light switch being flicked on and off. The lights were there and, just as suddenly, gone.

From out of nowhere I heard my own voice yelling at Heather. "Pull over the car!"

"No," she said. "You don't know who they are! They could be killers and want to cut us up and put us in the trunk. I'm not pulling over!"

I yelled at her again, "Pull over the damn car now…it's not you they want it's me!" *Why did I say that?* I thought. I went to reach for the steering wheel with my left hand but at that moment Heather's head tilted and she looked like she was in a trance as she pulled the car over to the side of the road. Suddenly we were engulfed in bright white light. I looked around to the back seat and saw Stewart, Sally and Heather's son all lying still as if they were in a drug-induced sleep.

My mind went blank as I watched the light fill every corner of my vision. Where was it coming from? As I sat in the front seat I wondered what the hell was going on. Everyone was completely still. By this time our car was on the shoulder of the road and had come to a complete stop. I looked behind the car and saw that the big balls of light were there again. As I turned to look at the front of the car I found my answer. A very bright disc-shaped craft was on the road. I could see a doorway to the craft was open with beings walking off it towards the car. My heart began to pound so hard; I thought I was going to die right there.

Do not be afraid, I kept hearing in my head. *Do not be afraid. Get out of the car.* I reached for the door handle and slowly opened the car door. It was like watching my body; I had no control. *Why am I getting out of the car?* I thought. It was like I was standing beside myself watching what I was doing while my brain couldn't communicate with my body. I lost all free will. It was cold outside the car and there was mist in the air. Heat came from the craft that sat on the road in front of me. I stood motionless, waiting, as about six of them came walking toward me. They looked small, almost childlike, with big round black eyes.

Stay calm we will not harm you, I kept hearing but I did not see anyone speak to me. After a moment, two of them came up to me and told me to close the door of the car and go with them. They led me by the hands. I felt entranced looking at their huge dark eyes. Their hands were slightly cold to the touch and I remember thinking, *Where are they taking me?* For some reason I was not speaking to them verbally. It seemed that when we both spoke it was through some kind of telepathy. They led me across to the left hand side of the road and as I looked up I saw another craft. This one was larger than the one on the road. There, in the doorway, I saw them: two tall beings with blond hair and brilliant, large blue eyes.

In a rather rude manner I asked them, *What are you doing here? Can't you leave me alone?* I then asked myself, *What the hell am I saying?* As I approached the entrance the small beings let go of my hands and I simply walked onto the craft. I knew that this was not the first time I had met the Tall Blonds; how and when we met before was confusing to me in that moment.

What happened in the following hours started me on a life long journey to find truth, peace, acceptance and understanding of this experience. Some of the time I spent with them was clear in my mind from that moment forward. Other parts would take weeks, months and even years to come into clear focus. The events that transpired, as well as what I was shown and told inside the craft that fateful day, eventually returned to my consciousness.

My time with them came to an end and the craft landed so that I could be taken back to the car. I had no idea how long I'd been gone and my thoughts turned to my friends. I was led back to the car by the short beings and told to take my shoes off and put them in the back seat. *We do not want you to remember that you left the car yet and your feet are wet,* they told me. So, just as before, in an almost hypnotic state, I did as I was told. The car door closed and I sat watching the little ones go back onto the craft. With a flash it lifted straight up and quickly vanished. As they left, my mind became free and my thoughts were my own again. They were no longer sharing my headspace.

The second the craft and the balls of light were gone everyone in the car began to stir.

The conversation was very normal for such a strange night. Stewart asked, "Why are we stopped? Did you want me to drive again?"

"Yes," said Heather, as she shifted around in her seat. "What time is it?" she asked but never got a reply. The four of us traded seats. Stewart complained to Heather about turning the car off because it was so cold. I jumped into the back seat and the conversation turned to the strange lights that had been following us for hours. Heather started talking about the radio that kept coming on with the strange station. Sally told us she had also noticed the radio fading in and out for a long time and also noticed the strange lights. We all thought it was quite strange. I asked Sally why she didn't tell us about the lights when we had switched drivers. Neither she nor Stewart answered.

The car wasn't running so Stewart started it. He said he didn't wanted to talk about the lights anymore and insisted we all stop talking about them. He pulled the car out onto the road and as he did the lights shone onto the left shoulder of the highway. *There they are!* I thought, *Now they can all see them.* "Look!" I shouted. "Look at that on the side of the road!" There were at least 5 sets of big glowing eyes staring back at us.

"It's deer Miriam!" Stewart shouted.

"No it's not!" I said. "Look at them! They're not deer! Can't you see them?" He kept arguing with me and explained that deer come down from the mountains to eat on the shoulder of the road because that is where the best grazing is. "Why are they standing so close together?" I asked. Everyone in the car began to get mad at me. "Don't you remember the lights? What the hell is going on?" I said. As we drove past I asked, "Why would they all be standing beside that house with all the floodlights on?" I tried to get Stewart to stop the car and look at them but we began to argue and he got very angry. He told me and everyone else to shut-up about it, saying that if I didn't stop talking he would stop the car and make me walk home. Heather and Sally yelled at me to please let it go. Afraid Stewart may lose his temper, I reluctantly stopped talking. Not a single word was said by anyone in the car until we arrived back in Vancouver and pulled into the driveway.

The sun was beginning to rise and a thin light was filtering into the dark sky as the car rolled to a stop in front of our home. It was the first time anyone had said a word in hours. The conversation began with everyone talking about how great it was to be home. Quickly the conversation changed to the strange lights that we all saw. Everyone had their own ideas as to what they thought it was that happened on the drive.

Stewart laughed and said, "Who knows maybe it was a UFO. Do we have any missing time?"

"What do you mean?" I asked.

"When Aliens take you and spend time with you, you can't account for the time you were with them." He looked at his wristwatch just as he approached the door to the house. Looking up with a smile he chuckled gleefully and said, "Nope, it took thirteen hours, just as long as usual."

I walked into the house with my bags and took them up to my room. As I took my coat off I looked down at my favourite beige shirt. There was some sort of black smear on it. As soon as I noticed it I slipped back into a robotic state. I took the shirt off and put it directly in the garbage. Not only did I put it in the garbage but I also took it to the bin outside. *Why?* I kept asking myself even as I was doing it: it was my favourite shirt. *Why not try to clean it?* Even Sally tried to get me to attempt to clean it first, but I got angry with her so she dropped the subject.

After disposing of the shirt I went back up to my room. There was a dull ache on the right side of my abdomen. When I looked down at the area I noticed a round red spot about two inches in diameter. In the center there was what appeared to be an incision. Once again I heard a voice in my head. It was telling me, *Do not to look at it again. Leave it alone and it will go away. There is no need to be concerned.* I put my nightshirt on and didn't look at it again for months.

I slept most of the next day recuperating from the long drive. I had strange dreams and saw the man and woman again. When I awoke I began to write down everything I remembered from the night before. When I wrote I started remembering many of the things they told me. *You will remember this, you will remember,* they had said just before they took me go back to the car. The Tall Blond Aliens looked into my eyes with their bright blue eyes and white, translucent skin as they repeated the message, *You will remember this.*

So much of the information in my mind didn't make sense but I knew it was important to write it down. It was as though they had downloaded information into my mind and I had to look at each piece and then find the appropriate place to file it. The whole experience was overwhelming.

Overnight I became a completely different person. I stopped drinking, smoking, partying and eating red meat. Everyone I knew kept telling me how different I seemed and how they were concerned. Prior to that night I had never meditated. Now I found myself in meditation two to three times a day, during which I sometimes saw the man and woman from my past encounters. At times I saw other beings that gave me a great deal of spiritual knowledge. It was always an enlightening experience to go into a deep meditation.

From the moment I woke from my nap after we arrived back in Vancouver, one thing was clear: my psychic ability was wide open. It was as though the Tall Blond Aliens gave me the gift of sight: a sight so far reaching that I could never in a lifetime explain to someone what I saw and understood about our world and the universe. It was the most beautiful gift I could ever have been given. On the other hand it was difficult to maintain the level of awareness they gave me in a world that has no place for such insightfulness.

I gave a lot of thought as to how long I spent with those beings in the days after seeing them. Finally, I realized one important fact about our trip. We drove for thirteen hours but we didn't stop like we normally did to let Stewart sleep for three hours. We had two drivers and we didn't make any extra stops than usual on our trip home. We should have been home after ten hours. We had three hours of missing time.

Not everything was completely clear. What did they do to my stomach where the redness was? Why couldn't I remember that part of what happened? Some of the details were fuzzy; yet the message remained clear. My job was to educate others about who they were.

Strange memories began to resurface from my childhood that implied my father knew who these beings were. Some of the things he talked about when we were kids made me think he was very familiar with who these beings were.

Months after seeing the Aliens I still had telepathic communication with them. One afternoon as I was walking down Granville Street, from out of nowhere I heard the voice of one of the Aliens booming in my head directing me to enter a jewellery store.

I opened the door to the store and entered. *Walk straight ahead,* they said and so I followed the request. With no hesitation I was directed straight to a counter, told to turn right and look down. *You need to buy the necklace, it is important to you.*

Two identical necklace pendants sat there, one blue and one red. *Which one?* I asked in my mind? Personally I liked the red one, ruby, but I was directed to buy the blue one, which was sapphire. Both of the pendants were rather dainty with nine small points that made the shape of a star. I didn't question why they asked me to purchase the necklace. I had enough prior contact with them to know there must be a good reason.

I knew I only had one hundred and ten dollars and not a dime more. I asked the clerk what the cost was. My heart sank when she told me it was one hundred and thirty dollars, before tax. *Do not concern yourself with the cost, she will give it to you as it was meant to be,* the voice boomed. I looked at the clerk and explained that I couldn't afford it. She then surprisingly lowered the price. Again, I had to tell her I didn't have enough money. She finally looked at me and asked how much money I had; I told her I only had one hundred and ten dollars. I was shocked when she told me that it was enough and that she would give me a gold chain as well!

I walked out of the store onto the street with the blue star pendant around my neck. In my mind I asked the Aliens what it meant and why I was instructed to buy it. They replied, *It is a blue star and it is very important to you, one day you will understand its full meaning. It is sacred and it is important to many people in the future. It will help you remain close to us.*

Once the necklace went on my neck I never took it off. It became a symbol to me of everything I knew to be the truth. That truth was clear: human beings are not the only intelligent life on the planet and, one day, everyone would know that as well.

MEMORIES RETURN

Within a very short period of time after my abduction I began to see flashes of my childhood that I either didn't understand before or had completely forgotten about until after seeing the Aliens. These images were very clear in my mind and no matter what I did I couldn't seem to set them aside. It was obvious that I was meant to have these memories return to my consciousness. How all the pieces of these memories fit into the whole picture of what I was experiencing wasn't yet clear to me. All I knew was that each piece was just as important as the next.

IN MY CRIB
(1966)

One of the first memories to return to me only days after I saw the Aliens was of me as a baby. I remembered lying in my crib, looking up at the ceiling, unable to talk or move much. The faces of three Aliens with big black eyes looked down on me.

AGE FOUR OR FIVE
(1970-1971?)

It was the middle of the night and I was about four or five years old. I awoke and walked out of my bedroom into the living room of our small house. My oldest sister, Janice, followed me into the living room. She kept telling me to get back into bed. I ignored her and proceeded to go outside, walking out into the farmer's field that was directly in front of our home. Janice tried everything to get me back to bed. She said it was late and that we would get into trouble. I walked about 15 feet into the field and stopped; Janice stood about three feet to the left of me. On the other side of the field we could see a very big bright light, about forty feet across, hovering silently above an old shed.

We both stood very still, staring. As we watched a blue ball of light the size of a baseball came out of the center of the hovering light. It flew across the field towards us so fast that I thought it would hit me and make a hole right through me. It stopped six inches from me in the center of my body where it hovered for a moment. Then it moved slowly down to my feet before returning to my forehead. It then came to rest at the middle of my body. After it was done with me, it slowly moved to Janice and did the exact same thing. When it finished it went back up to Janice's forehead where it sent a blue beam of light into her head; then she simply turned and went back to the house without saying a word. When she was gone I heard a voice in my head telling me to go with them.

The next thing I remember I was onboard the craft with Tall Blond Aliens. I was in the sitting position in what could be described as a chair that appeared to be made of light. Light was all around me—it was all I could see except for any Aliens that were within two or three feet of me. I was strapped down somehow but I couldn't see any straps. My arms were bent in a forty-five degree angle with my palms up. I screamed in agony! There were needles with small tubes coming out of them in both my arms, about two inches above my wrists. I couldn't see to what the tubes were attached. It felt like I was being blown-up like a balloon and it was terrifying! The Tall Blonds stood beside me, telling me to try to stay calm: it would be over soon. They said they had to change my blood so that I would be protected from diseases that would be coming in the future. I found it reassuring when they spoke; their voices not only calmed me but somehow eased my pain from the needles as well.

After they finished changing my blood they let me walk around the craft and look out the windows. It was very interesting. I watched as they sent out probes (known today as orbs), which, I was told, all had different jobs to do. Some were sent out to collect data from the air, water and soil and bring physical samples back to the craft for testing. Others, I was told, would be sent out to look for someone specific if they had to pick them up. Since the probes were small they could go into an area more easily than a craft. If someone they were looking for had other people with them the probes would be sent down to help put them to sleep by sending out a sound tone signal that would make everyone unconscious. Some of the probes collected information on specific people or on specific areas of interest.

I was allowed to watch from the window as the craft landed on the Earth, but I was not allowed to go outside. I have no idea where we were but it was night and it looked like a huge grassy field. Outside I saw at least four other craft in a circle. People and Aliens began to emerge from the crafts and gather outside. I wanted to go and join them but I was told I was too young. They did, however, tell me it was a meeting between Aliens and people to talk about the future and share information. There were some average-looking people there but I saw at least two men who looked like they were in some sort of uniform: possibly military types. They told me that one day in the future I would be able to attend one of these meetings.

When the Aliens took me back home I was given an object to take with me. They told me that it was very important and that I must remember it. This gift would some day be important to my future. I was told to bury it and when I was older and I knew what it was for I was to go back and find it.

When I got back to my bedroom I went straight to sleep; it wasn't until the next day that I took the object outside to bury it. Janice was with me at the time and I showed her but wouldn't let her touch it. I wrapped it in a white cloth before putting it in the earth. I told her we had to hide it from our father; if he found it he might destroy it or keep it from me.

AGE TEN
(1976)

One morning I awoke and began to walk down the hallway towards the kitchen. As I did a strange dream from the night before came into my mind. Janice and my mom were sitting at the kitchen table; my dad was out of town. My middle sister, Carol, was still in bed. I told my mom and sister about the really strange dream I had had about a UFO landing behind the house. Incredibly, they had both had the same dream as I! When Carol awoke we asked her if she had had any dreams the night before.

"Yes, actually, it was really weird. I had a dream that there was a UFO behind the house."

None of us remembered much of anything other than the craft in the backyard. This incident was very uncanny. We sat together and had a long discussion about how we could have all had the same strange dream. There was no explanation.

I was in grade five in 1976 and my teacher at the time was Mrs. Baxter. I really liked her as my teacher. Shortly after that night, for apparently no reason, I became terrified of her. She had huge round eyes and when she was expressing herself her eyes would become so big that it looked like they would pop out of her head. I couldn't look at her anymore! She scared the hell out of me when her eyes opened so wide.

For a long time after having the UFO dream both of my sisters would torment me by making their eyes as wide as they could. I would scream in terror, running from them, begging them to stop! Sometimes they would laugh at me because I was so afraid. It was rather easy to get me to do anything they wanted. All they had to do was threaten me with bulging eyes and I would do as they asked just to stop them; it was awful!

During this same time period I would walk in my sleep a lot, get bleeding noses and have night terrors that left me feeling like I was paralyzed. In order for me to go to sleep I would have to have all the doors closed; if there was even the slightest crack of an opening in the curtains I couldn't sleep. I always felt like someone would be watching me from the window, or hiding under my bed or closet.

AGE TWELVE
(1978)

In 1978 there was a boy at school whom all the girls liked. He was very cute and his name was Sam. My very good friend, Gillian, was dating him. I remember having a conversation with another friend, Trish, about him. I clearly remember Trish telling me that she wanted to have his baby! I don't think we even really understood what we were saying at the time. We were too young.

It was lunchtime and raining so most of the kids were inside. The hallway was full of kids and as we passed the gym I could see the grade seven class practicing basketball. I walked with Trish and said, "I will never have children! EVER!"

"Why not Miriam?" she asked.

"I will never have children because I don't think it will be human! I think it would be a monster or an Alien or something!"

Trish thought this was an odd thought to have about having kids. For most of lunch we talked about why I had such a strange thought. I never managed to explain to her with any clarity why I felt as I did but it was a strong and frightening feeling.

AGE SIXTEEN
(1982)

Every once in awhile Darren, my boyfriend, and I would go for a drive for something to do. When you live in a small town, going for a drive is a form of entertainment. It was always nice to get out of the glow of the town's lights to look at the stars.

One night Darren, his friend Ron and I went for a drive on one of the old logging roads. Ron drove while I sat in the middle with Darren beside me. We stopped the car on the side of the dirt road about five miles out of town. As we got out of the car we were talking and looking around the area. On the horizon there was a ridge—I wouldn't call it a mountain, rather it was a steep hill in the distance. It was very dark and the stars were visible; it was beautiful. The three of us stepped towards the front of the car to stand and talk when Ron said, "What was that?" I was facing the front of the car, Ron was to my right and Darren was to my left. I did see something out of the corner of my eye to the right but I missed exactly what it was.

"Wow! Did you see that one?" Darren asked. I had caught it that time!

"It looks like a meteor shower!" said Ron.

As we all watched the show of lights, I remember clearly that I was confused by it. We argued about what it was we were watching. The lights that went streaking down behind the ridge were very bright and appeared to be white balls of light, some with red tails on them. After watching this for about a minute the lights began to get brighter as they shot from the sky to the Earth. Every time they completely changed direction at the last second to travel parallel to the Earth and then streak out of sight.

"How can it be meteors when they don't go down behind the ridge? Meteors don't change directions!" I shouted, getting angry with them as they kept arguing with me. I yelled at them again, "Look at that one! It went straight down and when it got to the ridge it changed direction and traveled parallel with the Earth. That is not a meteor! What the hell is it!?"

That was the last thing I remember until we were all getting back into the car. Each of us was in a confused state as we drove back into town. The night was cold and we turned the heat on in the car, confused by how the car had become so cold so fast—we had only been out of it for a few minutes. Once we arrived back at our apartment we talked about what we saw. None of us remembered how long we had been out there. It was as though our memories had been wiped clean.

It was around this time that I fell very ill. I remember that I felt fine one day and the next I was so sick I could barely walk. Within three days I was so sick that Darren had to take me to the doctor's office. He had to carry me because I was so weak I could barely walk. My doctor at the time had no idea what would be causing me to be so sick since my symptoms didn't indicate any common malady.

She sent me for a blood test around the corner from her office. Darren and I barely made it there. I had to quickly lie down or I would have fallen over. They tried to take my blood but it was extremely difficult. I remember the nurses being in shock at how ill I was. They asked how long I had been in this condition and I told them that I was fine three days prior. They kept poking me with that darn needle but they couldn't get any blood. My veins kept collapsing. I knew that wasn't good! The nurse told me that if they couldn't get a blood sample they would have to send me to the hospital. Finally they drew some blood. It was a very small amount and they weren't sure it was enough for the tests they needed to run. I went home with the advice of my doctor that if I got any worse to go to the hospital.

A couple of days later the blood work came back normal for everything they tested. Baffled, my doctor told me she had no explanation at all and by the end of the week I was completely healthy again!

A short time after our experience on the logging road I began to have pains on my right side. This went on for months and, again, the doctors had no explanation. The pain became more and more intense as time went on. They did so many tests on me that I felt like I was being used for experiments. After I arrived in the Hospital Emergency on several occasions because of the pain, they finally decided to do exploratory surgery to see what was going on. When the doctors did the surgery they found a cyst the size of a grapefruit on my right ovary.

I wondered if that was a result of that night on the dirt road with Ron and Darren. All I know is that my right ovary has given me nothing but problems since that time, to the present day. Coincidence? Maybe. The fact remains that meteors do not change direction and then travel parallel to the earth. The events that followed the night with Darren and Ron left me confused. I may never remember what happened that night with the "meteors" but, by my body's reaction to it, maybe it's best that I don't.

* *

These returning memories were crystal clear in my mind after I saw the Aliens on the highway in 1988. I thought that if I kept writing everything down, the full picture would become clear. Perhaps the messages they gave me were somehow intertwined with these memories. Only time would tell and all I was trying to do was stay as sane as possible while the information poured out of me.

I really wanted to ask Janice about seeing the Aliens when we were young but that would have to wait. It was important that I didn't tell her any details of the event, as I wanted her to remember completely on her own. If I said anything specific it would cloud her memory and I would always question whether her memories were real or not. If I kept the details to myself and she remembered on her own then I would know the memories were real and not my imagination. Only time would reveal the Alien secrets.

CLONES
(1989)

I was alone for nine months looking for someone, anyone, who knew
something about Aliens. I felt confused with all of the feelings and memories that had surfaced since the highway trip. Aliens were always in the
forefront of my mind; I felt like I was going insane. Every week, it seemed,
I was visiting places I had never dreamed of being only a short time before.
During those first 9 months I went to the Theologian Society, a meeting
of the Rosicrucian Order, various psychics, metaphysical meetings, Bud-
dhist Temples, spiritual bookstores and countless other places. Everywhere
I went it was always the same: no one could tell me anything. Yet they were
all fascinated with my story and wanted to hear what the Aliens had told
me. Without any confirmation of the things I had been told and shown, I
was left searching for the truth to my experiences on my own.

I asked Anna to come with me to a spiritual bookstore I had heard about in
Surrey, a suburb of Vancouver. I had to make the long trip by bus in hopes of
finding someone who maybe had some answers. When we arrived I scanned
the posted notes on the wall, looked for flyers and booklets of upcoming meetings and asked the person working there if they had any books on UFOs.
The man told me there were only a couple. Fascinated, he told us that in the
previous few months people had begun to ask for books on the topic. I told
him that he should get some books in because more and more people would
begin to search for any information they could find on Aliens and UFOs. I
told him that I had been all over the city in my search for confirmation of my
experiences and that this bookstore was one of my last resorts. Then I gathered
a small pile of flyers and Anna and I headed back into the city.

Back in my apartment I read through the pile of papers, searching for any
new groups, meetings, or signs of anyone who might be able to help me. A
notice in a spiritual paper caught my attention. It read, "Attention all Star
People." I remember the moment clearly: my heart jumped and I began cry-

ing. *Finally*, I thought, *maybe I'm not crazy after all!* Seeing my reaction, Anna quickly read the notice and encouraged me to call the phone number listed. It was a Seattle number, but that meant little to me at that moment.

I felt faint as my hand reached for the telephone and dialled the number. When a woman answered, I told her nervously about the advertisement I had seen. Her name was Karen and she quickly put me at ease as I began to share some of my experiences from the highway. After I spoke, she shared some of her knowledge with me. I felt comfortable enough to tell her some of the things the Aliens had told me. For the next two hours I cried as Anna sat beside me, holding my hand in support. Karen was the saviour of my soul and my mind. She helped me realize that I was completely sane when she validated my memories. She confirmed that I was not alone in these experiences and assured me they were real and not imagined. She thought I was in need of some emotional support and suggested I come to Seattle to see her so we could talk more about our experiences in person.

Two days later I was in the Vancouver Greyhound Bus depot, waiting to catch a bus to Seattle. I gave all the information I had on Karen to Anna in case I was not right about my feelings with Karen—perhaps I was in fact heading to meet a crazy person. I was nervous about going to the United States because, up until that point in my life the only places I had ever been were Cranbrook and Vancouver. I found my desire to find answers was strong enough to crush any fear I had.

The four-hour long bus ride gave me time to think and relax before I met the only people I knew who had information on UFOs. I was nervous and, at the same time, calm. It was a rather strange sensation. Once in Seattle the bus dropped me at a hotel where I called Karen to let her know I had arrived. She told me to stay put while she sent her husband to pick me up.

I stood at the entrance of the hotel wondering what these people would be like. I felt happy to have found them yet still a little nervous. Karen's husband arrived a short time later and we drove together back to their home. Karen greeted us at the front door; we hugged as I cried in relief to be meeting her in person.

I entered the small house where I was welcomed by three of Karen's friends. It took no time at all for all of us to begin talking freely. Although

I didn't feel comfortable enough to tell them every detail, I shared with the small group the events that led me to them and was surprised to hear that all of them had had similar experiences to mine. We talked until well past midnight about how each of us had been informed that we had a certain mission to complete. The conversation put me at ease. I no longer felt alone and meeting these people showed me that I was definitely on a new path in life. I knew then that nothing would ever be the same again.

Before leaving the next day Karen gave me the phone number of a man she had met, John Davis, who lived in Vancouver. She suggested I give him a call. Apparently he had a great deal of information on the subject of UFOs and Aliens. When I asked her how she and John had met, she told me he had found her advertisement as well. They visited on a couple of occasions. She didn't have a lot of background on him—but he lived in Vancouver, so he was close to me.

I was so excited to call John and did so almost immediately after arriving home. During our telephone conversations I found him to be friendly and well informed. Within a short time we decided to meet in person, as I was eager to begin a friendship with him. I was thrilled to finally have a contact that I could relate to close to home.

John and I met in a coffee shop and we talked about my experience for hours. We spent the entire afternoon together walking and sharing with each other the knowledge we had acquired. I learned that he worked for a small company that installed super computer systems. Apparently there were eight men that worked in his office and they were a tight group, all with interests in UFOs.

From the first time I met John in person I had the feeling that he wasn't completely up-front with me about what he knew. He seemed to be holding back something but I couldn't put my finger on it. John had a very unique look: short, dark hair—almost black, combed to one side. He wore thick glasses over black eyes and had a strange olive tone to his skin. He often wore a beige pair of pants with pockets on the sides—similar to cargo pants of today but at the time I had never seen anyone wearing these type of pants.

John and I spent a lot of time together and it was because of him I was able to make new contacts in the city. He gave me the name of a woman named Sandra Jones. He told me he hadn't met her personally but heard from his friends that she was an excellent contact to have. Sandra and I quickly became good friends. She had an ability to gather people together like I have never seen before. It was as though she had her finger on the pulse of the city. It was partly due to her influence that I was able to start abductee meetings in an attempt to bring people like myself together.

All sorts of people would show up for these meetings, including some really crazy people with claims I never believed. These meetings didn't last long but gave me the initial support and acceptance of which I was in desperate need. I found a few others like myself at the gatherings. However, I found the attention I drew to myself overwhelming; strange things began happening around me and I made the decision to stop the meetings after only a few months.

My friendship with John grew and I was happy to have friends who I could relate to. Although I spent a lot time with John, I never fully trusted him. I pushed those feelings aside and kept a little distance from him by not always sharing all my information. He seemed very secretive about certain aspects of his life so I always knew that something wasn't right.

With so many new people in my life, it made the year disappear in the blink of an eye and before I knew it 1989 came to an end.

RUSSIAN RECRUITING
EARLY (1990)

The year was 1990 and I was working in a yogurt shop. With everything that was going on around me I was happy that my job didn't have many expectations. When business was slow the owner would sometimes have an employee work alone. Such was the case this day. I was trying to keep busy so the hours would slip by quickly. The small lunch crowd came and went and time was now ticking by slowly.

The shop was empty when a man passed the window at the side of the shop. He looked directly at me, smiled, and then walked around to the front of the store and in the front door. He wore a long black coat and had dark, slightly curly hair, with a beard and deep brown eyes.

He walked straight up to the counter and said with a smile, "Do you work for the CIA or the FBI?"

"No," I replied. *Damn, I thought to myself, what the hell is going on now? Maybe if I just play stupid, he'll leave. Maybe, just maybe, it's a joke!*

"Have you ever worked for the CIA or the FBI?" he asked without missing a beat.

"No," I said, trying to laugh him off. His next question took my breath away, but I managed to hold my composure.

"Have you ever thought about working with the Russians? They work with people like you, you know."

"No, I'm not interested, thanks," I replied with a blank stare.

"You would be around people like yourself, people that understand you, we could help you to control your abilities."

Once again I said, "I'm not interested, thanks."

" Do you know how powerful you are?" he asked.

"Yes I do actually!" I said as I glared into his eyes. I was already shielding myself from his stare so he couldn't look further into me with his psychic ability.

"Yes, but can you control it?" he asked.

"Yes I can actually!"

He then said, "If you're ever interested we would like to have you come and work with us. We have about 10,000 people like you that we work with. You would never have to feel like you are alone again."

"I am not interested now and will never be interested in the future. Please go back to who sent you here and tell them thank you for their interest, but there is no point in ever sending someone again. No matter what happens I will never be interested!"

The man, who never gave me his name, simply said, "Thank-you," and left the store. For the next three days he came in for yogurt but never brought up the subject again. On the third day I asked him how he found me. He evaded my question and left quickly, never to be seen again.

BLUE-EYED LADY
MIDDLE (1990)

It was the last weekend before the school year started. The evening was warm and Robson Street was busy with people. There were four of us behind the small serving counter where I worked and it was quite apparent that everyone was craving frozen yogurt. There was no time for chitchat between workers since the line-up stretched out onto the street.

I had my back to the door when an overwhelming urge to turn and look at the entrance swept over me. Walking in the door was a very odd-looking woman. With no hesitation I asked, *Why are you here?* Panic swept over me: something was not right about this situation. *Why can't you leave me alone? Can't you see I'm working!*

She seemed to work her way through the crowd with great ease and no one noticed her. How could they not? She was so strange in her appearance.

She wore layer upon layer of beige clothing and was completely clothed from head to toe while everyone else wore shorts. A colourful scarf was pulled snugly around her chin so that none of her neck was exposed. She stood 6 ½ feet tall, towering above the crowd and had the shoulders of a football player. The tone of her skin was not normal either, appearing very mask-like. Her blond hair hung down below her shoulders, pulled towards her face. It looked more like a wig than natural hair. She was extremely ugly except for her large, brilliant blue eyes, which seemed to control me. I felt incredibly uncomfortable. She made her way to the counter in front of me as though waiting to be served. *Just a minute, I'll serve you next!* The entire conversation was through telepathy.

I felt irrational in my thoughts, questioning if this was really happening to me or had I finally lost my mind? After my last transaction was finished I walked over to the strange woman. I had several questions for her and I was determined to find the answers. *Why are you here to check up on me? As you can see this is what I have to do to survive in this world! Is this the reason for your visit, to see what I do for work?* She was silent. I looked around the room wondering how could it be that no one noticed her. *Perhaps this is my imagination,* I thought, *perhaps I am crazy.* I knew I could never tell anyone about this woman or they would lock me up for sure.

Don't tell me, you want strawberry yogurt! I got the small dish and turned my back to her for a moment. When I looked at her again she had moved down to the end of the counter. It was then that I saw the full view of her. She looked ridiculous! The beige suit looked like it was from the 1970s, it was heavy and covered her entire body. *Look at yourself! You look so out of place*! She took a step back and examined her clothing. *The next time you decide to visit someone, try not to look so out of place!*

I put the yogurt cup down on the counter and asked sarcastically, *Do you have money to pay for it?* Her response came as a shock to me. From within her suit pocket she retrieved an old two-dollar bill and set it on the counter. *Don't you have any new money, or is this all you have?* I asked. *Next time you go and see someone you should get* some *new clothes as well as money so you don't look so out of place!* I made the transaction and put the change on the counter so I would not have to touch her. Slowly her hand reached toward the counter to retrieve the change. Her hand was half the width of a normal hand and the fingers were long and skinny, almost like pinchers. The flesh was off-white with a slight pinkish, somewhat transparent tone.

I stood in shock as I watched her glide through the crowd with great ease and out onto the street. It seemed like the crowd moved out of her way without a word being spoken. Awakening from my trance-like state of mind, my rational thinking rushed back to me. The woman hadn't uttered a single word. What had just happened? Why had it happened? I wanted the answers but held back a strong urge to run out onto the street after her.

Quickly I asked a co-worker, "Did you see that?"

"See what?" she asked.

"My last customer?"

"No I didn't," she replied. Frantically, I went from person to person asking if they had seen her. One girl said she remembered seeing a very tall, blond woman but didn't notice anything out of the ordinary. There seemed to be no point in questioning them any further.

My immediate conclusion while trying to rationalize the woman's visit was that I had lost my grasp on reality. I told myself that I would never tell anyone about the incident. Perhaps all the talk about Aliens had begun to play tricks on my mind. I tried to relax for the rest of my shift but found it difficult to keep my mind off of the woman.

Several weeks prior I had been drawn to buy *Transformation*, Whitley Strieber's book, despite the fact that I had no desire to read the book. I normally didn't read books on the subject but something compelled me to make the purchase. The book found a home in the corner of my apartment where it remained until one week after the encounter at the yogurt shop.

That afternoon I got home feeling extremely tired and had intended on resting. From across the room, *Transformation* caught my eye. I walked over, picked it up and began to read. After only a couple of chapters I questioned why I was reading the book since nothing in it was of interest to me. Yet for some reason I was unable to put it down. It was not until the early hours of the next morning when I could stay awake no longer that I closed it up and got some rest.

From work the next day I hurried home, eager to finish the book. One of the last chapters, "Visitors Emerge," brought me to tears. It was then that I realized why I was compelled to read this book. More importantly, I realized that I was not crazy.

"Visitors Emerge" was a detailed account of two separate incidents in which physical contact was made with extraterrestrials. What set these contacts apart were the locations in which they took place. These Alien visitations had settings in full view of other people. The Aliens seemed to make no clear attempt to hide, and were able to walk among us free of detection by the general population.

In both cases in the book the details were strikingly similar to my encounters. In one case the Alien description was almost identical to mine, including the beige suit and scarf pulled up over the chin. The Alien was seen by the observer simply walking past her with a copy of *Transformation* in her arms.

I cried for some time after reading the book as I realized that for whatever reason, the Aliens had made a special visit to see me. Once again I found myself asking, *Why me? Who am I?*

LATE (1990)

I was preparing myself to tell my father about meeting the Aliens. I knew he would be in Vancouver so I contacted him to tell him that I had something important I needed to talk about. He agreed to see me when he next came to the city. We'd never had a close relationship so I knew speaking with him wouldn't be easy. When he finally arrived we set up a meeting on Commercial Drive. We sat in the booth of a cheap restaurant, drinking coffee, and talked for a short time.

My father has a strong personality and normally wouldn't allow someone to tell him what to do for any reason. I began to get nervous thinking about how I could explain what happened on the highway with the Aliens. Anxiously, I shifted in my seat, played with a stray piece of paper and looked from my father to the table. Finally, I looked him straight in the eye and said, "I need to tell you about something that happened to me. I need you to listen to my whole story before you start asking me questions. Please wait until I tell you that you can speak before you start talking." Without further comment, to my surprise, he agreed.

Suspecting that somehow my father had his own experiences with Aliens, I thought I had put a small piece of the Alien puzzle together. But my suspicions were only speculation. After I told him my story, I knew he would confirm or deny the fact that he knew about them. Shaking, I relayed the story of my abduction on the highway that fall day in 1988. I then sat back and watched him. He didn't stir and he didn't say a word. I was still shaking and felt terrified as I waited for his response. "Why don't you say anything?" I asked.

He smiled and said, "You never told me I could speak." *My God!* I thought, *he does know!*

"Sorry, yes you can speak! What do you think?"

As long as I live I will not forget his response. He gently leaned in to me and very calmly but sternly said, "Those bastards, why didn't you tell me? The worst they ever were with me was 25 years ago!" A lightning bolt shot through my entire body as he confirmed his involvement. He asked again why I didn't tell him sooner.

"What good would that have done?" I asked.

"Maybe I could have stopped them! Those bastards!"

"How could you have done that?"

"I don't know! But I could have at least tried to stop them!" he growled back at me.

The only thing I told him that day was about my highway experience, nothing more. Yet that was enough to confirm that he knew all about the Aliens. He also confirmed that my memories as a baby of the Aliens over my crib were real, although I didn't tell him about them. I was almost 25-years old and yet he had only just shared that they were always around him at that same time. *Could it be possible that it wasn't my father they were seeking, but me? Is that why they were around all the time?* Another question to add to my already very long list.

It was getting late and I needed to go home to get ready for work the next day. We decided to meet the following day and talk some more about the whole experience.

This time we met at a pub for a drink where I began to tell him about the Russian who asked me to join their psychic program. He looked at me and, smiling, asked, "What did you tell them?"

"I told them I wasn't interested and never would be!"

He laughed out loud and said, "That's good, that's good!" as he kept laughing. "Why did you tell them you weren't interested?"

"I remembered the story you used to tell us when we are kids about never going with them if they ever approached me. You used to tell me that once you were on the streets of Paris during the war and a man approached you. You said this man asked you to go and work for what you called 'The Russian Psychic Army.' You used to tell me to *never* go with them. You would say, 'What do they think I'm stupid? You work for them, you can never leave; they will kill you and they own you. You can't hide! There is nowhere to hide on this planet, they are some of the strongest psychics in the world and they can find you with their minds. They don't need to use a gun to kill you; they do it with their minds. Don't ever go with them, do you understand!?' You told me this story so many times as a child that when the man asked me to work for the Russians, I knew he was serious!"

All my father did was laugh at this story. "Like father like daughter," he said and that was the end of our conversation about the Russians.

We sat together and talked for a couple of hours. I shared with him that since my encounter my psychic ability had become heightened; he said he wasn't surprised. Then out of the blue he leaned over to me and very aggressively said, "You are not an Alien, do you understand? You are not an Alien; you are my daughter and don't you ever forget that! No matter what anyone tells you, you are my daughter!" In that moment I knew I could never share with him everything the Aliens told me. His response would be to argue and I couldn't deal with that because I wanted to find out what he knew about them. If he got aggressive it would be impossible to get any information from him.

The conversation was waning and it wasn't long before my father and I parted ways. I didn't know it then but it would be years before we talked again. The meeting with him left me with even more questions regarding his involvement but it was also clear he didn't want to get involved. More importantly, it appeared to me that he didn't want *me* to get involved. My relationship with my father had always been strained.

John called me one night later that week and told me he wanted to show me something and hoped we could connect as soon as possible. I knew it must be important for him to want to meet so quickly so I saw him later that night. On the darkened street outside my boyfriend's apartment John and I sat on a street bench. He held in his hands an envelope from which he took out a document. He told me he got it from one of the guys he worked with. Although he wanted to share this document with me he warned me that if they found out he had shown it to me, he could be in a lot trouble. When I asked him why he was taking such a big risk he replied that he felt it was important for me to know its contents. The title of the document was "Protocol for Extraterrestrial Contact." There was reference to MJ12 on the cover page.

I took the document from him and went back to my boyfriend's place where Frank was waiting for me. We read the package together, barely able to believe our eyes. The information on those pages gave details as to how people who had contact with anything extraterrestrial would be dealt with. Specifically, it said they could be held by the government—isolated for any amount of time the government felt was needed. These people would have no contact with the outside world and would be held in quarantine indefinitely. It went on to mention certain families who were pre-chosen that would be taken to assigned areas in the case of Alien contact on a global scale. These families would have military protection from outsiders. There would be housing and supplies in order for them to live. They would be held in these camps in an attempt to save the human race in the event of a threat from extraterrestrials. The document went on and on in this manner.

I became afraid after reading the paper and Frank was clearly shaken as well. "What the Hell is going on?" Frank kept asking me. Sadly, I couldn't answer that question for him, let alone for myself. We wondered why John gave the MJ12 document to me to read and where he got it. Was he working for some government organization? That question played constantly in my mind.

I spent that night at Frank's apartment and we talked for a long time after reading the document, concerned about the implications for anyone who had had extraterrestrial contact. I kept thinking, *That's me! Maybe John was concerned for my safety and this was his way of warning me of the danger I may be in.* I fell asleep trying to put the pages out of my mind.

The next morning Frank had to go to work so I left with him and went back to my apartment. There I made a few calls to people whom I wanted to show the document. I knew John had asked me not to let anyone see it, but it was so important. I called a local researcher, Ted McDonald, whom I had made contact with through Sandra Jones the previous year. I told him I wanted to see him to ask his opinion on this MJ12 document. He sounded very excited about it on the telephone and we set up a meeting for later that day.

A couple of hours later I was on Robson Street in front of the Public Library. There I waited for Ted while I sat on a bench watching the tourists pass. The night before it had rained lightly and I was pleasantly surprised that the sun was shining. It didn't take long before Ted arrived and we began talking about the document. He told me he made an appointment to meet with another man as well as me. He said I didn't have to show the other man the document if I didn't feel comfortable, but Ted thought the two of us should meet.

As I pulled the papers out of the envelope I watched those around me. No one cares much about other peoples' business in the city but I didn't want to make a scene either. Near the top of the document "TOP SE-CRET" was stamped. Yet I kept thinking that it must be a joke of some kind. Just as Ted began to look at it he spotted his friend in the distance and jumped up to meet him.

As I waited for Ted to return I saw another man approaching. I recognized immediately that there was something very strange about him. He was dressed in an all black suit and had black hair. He had dark black sunglasses on even though the sun was not bright at the time. He walked past me very slowly and, as he passed, turned his head to look directly at me. He kept walking and then turned around to come back. There was a newspaper box in front of me, to the left. When he got in front of it he leaned over to look inside before turning, then looked directly at me and then back to the headlines. His movements were rigid and calculated, making him seem even more out of place.

Most disturbing was that, for some reason, I couldn't feel anything from him. I kept looking at him with his back turned, trying to make sense of the lack of any energy coming from him. Even when I look at a rock I feel some sort of energy emanating from it so it was extremely odd to watch this man and feel nothing. People consist of feelings; with this man it was as though he wasn't real—almost as though he was a hologram or an empty shell.

After a moment or two the man turned and walked straight over to me and stood directly in front of me, only inches from my knees. It was at that moment I realized, not only was this strange, but he was probably there because of me. He said in a monotone voice, "Do you know where there is any good shopping around here?" *What a stupid question!* I thought. We were surrounded by the best shopping district in Vancouver. I couldn't feel his presence even though he stood in front of me. If I had my eyes closed I wouldn't have known he was even there. I have been in a dead sleep when someone came to stand at my doorway and I sat straight up, looking right at them, knowing they were there because I could feel their energy, even in my sleep. That's how sensitive I am to peoples' energy. With this man, I felt *nothing.*

I turned the document over so he could see the "TOP SECRET" stamp: I wanted to get his reaction. At that moment Ted sat down beside me. We both watched as the man put his head down to look on my lap and, with no reaction at all, repeated his question. "Do you know where there is any good shopping around here?"

Very sarcastically I told the man, "I think you will find what you are looking for right here on Robson Street. All you have to do is turn around to find you are in the middle of the shopping district." He just stood there, not saying a word. Ted and I looked at each other and then I told the strange man, "You should go now, before all the stores close." He stood silently for at least two seconds and, without saying another word, he turned and walked away.

After he crossed the street Ted, his friend and I all shook our heads in disbelief over what just happened. "What did that man say to you?" Ted asked.

"He didn't say anything other than what you heard yourself."

"That was an MIB!" As usual, I knew nothing about what he was talking about. He explained to me that MIBs—Men In Black—were another part of the UFO phenomenon. No one really knows who or what these men are or what their purpose is. Interactions with them are usually brief and odd. They wear all black, often have dark sunglasses and have been known to drive very old black cars. This information made me nervous and only added to my already long list of strange occurrences around me since my highway encounter.

Ted and his friend were very taken aback, not only by the MIB, but also by my MJ12 document. They thought it must be genuine due to the strange interaction with the Man In Black. Ted tried to explain to me the little he knew about MJ12 but his information was limited. All he knew was that MJ12 was a group of 12 men who apparently had knowledge of the UFOs and were trying to gain control of the phenomenon. *(MJ12 is an interesting area in Ufology but my own knowledge is limited. It would be best for the reader to research the topic themselves for further information.)*

They wanted to make copies of the document but I heeded the words of John and didn't allow them to. If John was nervous about letting me see it and I was indeed just visited by an MIB then I felt it wouldn't be wise to make any copies. The three of us went for a coffee and discussed the afternoon's events where I found myself in the hot seat, feeling like I was playing 20 questions and explaining everything I knew about the Aliens to the two men. I got tired quickly and decided to say good-bye so I could go home and have John come and pick up the MJ12 document. I wanted it out of my hands!

Late that afternoon I received a call from Frank. He was very upset and clearly concerned. He told me the police had just left his home. Someone had broken into his apartment. Eerily, it seemed to the police that whomever had broken in was clearly looking for something in particular and that Frank's room was clearly the target of the break-in. His room and all its contents had been rifled through, including those in his closet. The kitchen, living room and his roommate's room were barely touched. The police thought my boyfriend was a drug dealer! There was about $10,000 worth of electric guitars and amps that weren't taken. An ounce of solid gold beside Frank's bed was also left untouched, as was money sitting in plain sight on his dresser.

Frank was, understandably, very upset by the break-in. I couldn't blame him as it upset me as well. He kept asking me what the Hell I was involved in and why they had targeted him. It seemed obvious to us both that it could have been someone looking for the document. I tried to calm Frank and downplay the events leading up to the break-in, but it didn't help.

It wasn't long before Frank told me he didn't want to see me anymore. How could I blame him? Ending the relationship broke my heart. I realized that from that point forward any relationship I did have would more than likely have complications. I always thought of myself as being a strong independent woman before all the Alien contact. With all the attention and experiences I was having I concluded it might be some time before I found someone to share my life with again.

END (1990)

By this time I was getting tired of all the craziness. There were so many questions I wanted answered for myself personally. At the same time, I seemed to already have many of those answers; I just needed to process all the information I had in my mind. It was a rather strange predicament to be in. When I talked about my experiences I often felt as though I was being interrogated. I was happy to share with others my experiences but they seemed to think I had the answers to everything and that was simply not the case.

One slow Saturday afternoon my co-worker and I sat chatting together. The day was rather cool and wet and the trickle of customers at the frozen yogurt shop made the minutes seem like hours. When a couple walked into the shop we both jumped to our feet to help serve them. They walked past my co-worker and looked directly at me. They kept eye contact and walked to the far end of the counter. I followed them, asking what I could get for them. After their first response, I knew they were there to see me.

Instead of ordering, the man began a strange conversation with me. He introduced himself and reached across the counter to shake my hand. He then introduced the woman with him. She reached across grabbed my hand and said, "It is an honour and a privilege to finally meet you." *What are these people really doing here? What does she mean,* finally *meet you?* I wondered.

During our conversation I found out they were from California and had apparently taken a last minute trip to Vancouver for only two days. The conversation was strange as it revolved around me. The man asked if I kept a journal. I told him that I did after which he told me that it would be important to me in the future and possibly for other people as well. *Strange comment!* I thought.

When I asked them about what they did for work the man told me they built new technologies for a company called Lockheed in California. All I could think as I stood there talking was, *Why? Why am I so important? Am I imagining all of this?* The two finally left—without any yogurt. (Years later I found out that, according to conspiracy theorists; reverse engineering of Alien technologies is done at Lockheed Martin in California.)

As the door closed behind them my co-worker walked over to me. "What did those people want? It was really weird, Miriam, it was as if they came in just to talk to you!" I tried my best to dispel her worries, but it did no good, she kept talking about them. From her observation it was as if they had led me to the end of the counter so they could talk to me alone. She said they looked creepy.

Everything in my life was like something out of a spy novel or science fiction movie. It was very difficult to handle and I wasn't sure how much more I could take as the number of bizarre incidents kept growing. I no longer wanted to be involved in the abductee meetings and was beginning to think that maybe I was too high profile. I could feel the real potential for danger to myself and I wasn't sure what to do about it.

I couldn't get the woman's words out of my mind: "It is an honour and a privilege to finally meet you." Who were they? And why did they come to see me? What did they know about me that I didn't? So many questions, and one answer only leads to more questions.

RUNNING AWAY

END (1990) BEGIN (1991)

I moved to Victoria in an attempt to remove myself from the spotlight. No longer could I tell myself that everything was okay when I knew it wasn't. Too many strange people popping into my life made my decision to leave Vancouver an easy one.

Some of my friends were beginning to feel that I might be in danger as well. Even though I was beginning to think the same thing, I tried to sway their thinking. The last thing I needed was for them to worry about me. I tried to get on with a normal life and keep to myself a little more. After the Russians, MIBs, Alien visitations, secret documents and break and enters I had had enough! It was time to leave and let some rational thinking seep back into my mind. I thought that the fireworks going on around me may calm down if I took a few steps back.

I got a job working at a car dealership washing cars. I was happy to have found such mindless work rather quickly. It gave me the opportunity to earn just enough to pay my bills yet not have much interaction with people. After all I had experienced the past two years, I was happy to have the quiet time.

I went to work one day and began washing the long line of new cars. On the street I saw a white van that was parked with a man sitting in the driver's seat. At first I thought maybe he was waiting to have work done on his van at the garage. As the day went on I began to question what he was doing there. He simply sat, looking straight ahead. Once in awhile he would turn his head and look directly at me for a moment and then turn his head to glare straight ahead again. After four hours I didn't see him eat or drink anything, nor did he leave the van at any point.

The back of the van had blacked-out windows which made me feel uncomfortable. By now I was a little paranoid—how could anyone blame me! I tried very hard to think of a rational explanation for his presence but found none. At around one in the afternoon I decided to go for lunch as it was a great opportunity to walk past the back of the van as close as I could and possibly see inside. As I passed the back window of the van the sunlight shone just right and I saw the outline of a long telescope camera! As I continued to walk, I became angry. I just wanted to be left alone! I came back from lunch to find the van and the man in the same position where they stayed for the entire day. At five in the afternoon I went home and left him there.

The following day the same van sat in the same position, but this time the driver was different. *How stupid do they think I am?* I kept thinking. Later that day, I saw an old black car, like the one my parents had when I was a child drive by. The driver wore all black, had black hair and wore dark sunglasses. He turned and looked directly at me as he passed by. I remembered what Ted told me about the MIBs and wondered if this was one of them. When he drove by a second time, only a matter of minutes later, he did as he had the last time—slowed the car down and looked directly at me, holding his glare. This time I smiled and waved at him, while thinking how much it ticked me off that he was there.

By this time I was very upset and wondered what was really going on with this van. I moved from Vancouver and stopped almost all contact with UFO people because all I wanted was to be left alone! So I took a deep breath and marched straight over to the man sitting in the driver's seat. "I noticed that you have been here all day, can I help you with something?" The man was surprised and I could see this on his face.

"No, thank you," he replied.

"Can I get you a coffee or something? I noticed you've been sitting here alone all day and you haven't even gone to the washroom. Can I get you anything?"

Clearly shaken by my actions he said, "No, thank you. I am fine."

I smiled and told him, "If you need anything just wave at me to let me know I will be watching for you." Then I walked away. After half an hour the van left and I never saw him again. Coincidence? Maybe. I was glad he was gone.

A couple of months later my friend Sandra from Vancouver called. When I left Vancouver I had asked her to let me know if she met anyone with a large amount of knowledge on UFOs, as I would be very interested in meeting with them.

She had met a man that seemed to be very interested in all areas of Ufology. When she met him she had mentioned my story to him and told him a little bit about me. He was apparently very interested in meeting with me. I was trying to keep a low profile but I didn't want to pass up the opportunity to meet with someone who was knowledgeable, so we set-up a time the following weekend for a meeting. I told them it would be easier for them to come to Victoria than for me to come to Vancouver.

It was midmorning on a sunny Saturday when they arrived. The house I was staying in was empty for the day so we didn't have to be concerned about any interruptions during our meeting. I was excited over the potential of finding another contact that would have knowledge similar to mine.

A car pulled into the driveway and I ran downstairs to the side door and went out to greet them. Sandra jumped out of the car and said hello while giving me a hug. The man was still fussing inside the car. When he stepped out and closed the door, my jaw dropped. *What the hell is going on?* I thought. The man, who introduced himself as Bill Walters, looked just like John Davis. His hair was the same colour and style, he had the same eyes, the same strange olive skin, thick big glasses and yes, even those same beige pants.

Immediately I was on guard. Obviously I was wrong in the assumption that I would be left alone by merely moving from Vancouver.

Over the next few hours we talked about a number of issues. Bill asked a lot of questions about what I was told and he especially wanted to know about Alien technology. I kept my answers as vague as possible since I felt I couldn't fully trust him. Maybe I was insane—who knew? I asked myself this question so many times that it was like having a recording on a loop in my head. At the first opportunity I got Sandra on her own and I told her about John Davis. Then I asked her how much she knew about Bill. Her knowledge was limited but she did say that he seemed to have a lot more information than most people did. As far as she knew he was a computer programmer whom she met at a UFO meeting. They quickly became friends and poof! there they were talking to me.

Throughout the day I attempted to get more information from Bill. Just like with John Davis, Bill was vague in many areas. I was frustrated by his lack of intent on sharing what he knew with me. It was clear as the day went on that he was aware that I was holding back with him.

Before heading back to Vancouver, Sandra and Bill suggested we have dinner. After we ate we all stood up to leave and Bill handed me his business card.

"You work with John Davis? I can't believe it!" I was incredulous—both John and Bill worked at the same computer company!

He looked at me blankly and said, "No. What do you mean?"

"You work with a guy named John Davis!" Still he insisted he did not know anyone named John. Quickly my fear turned to anger and I said, "Look! I know you work with John Davis in a small office with about eight other guys, you're all into UFOs and you work at a computer company installing super computers, so what the hell is going on here? Who are you!?"

Finally, he said, "Oh, right, John, yes I work with John, I am terrible with names, sorry."

Bill wouldn't go any further into how he knew John. He quickly paid for his dinner, stating that they had to run if they wanted to catch the ferry. "Call me if you ever come to Vancouver," he said. "I would really like to hear more of your story." As I watched them leave I stood motionless while my mind swirled with questions. *Who were these guys? I can concede that they both have the same occupation and even the same workplace; however, the fact that they both look the same and even wear the same strange beige pants is just a bit too much!*

(1991)

Over the next few months I went back to Vancouver a number of times and I called John on what had happened. As always, he seemed to have an answer for everything. Bill was forgetful, he said, and lived in his own headspace. As for them looking alike? He said that people did tell him that sometimes. The more I pressed, the less he talked. I also called Bill in an attempt to find out more. No one in my circle of friends ever met both Bill and John. I was the only one that knew them both. Some of the UFO people I knew met one or the other but only I had met both, which made it hard to convince people that I wasn't crazy!

My time in Victoria was short-lived as I was more comfortable living in Vancouver where I had my friends around me. After only six months I packed up and moved back. I was intent on keeping a low profile in an attempt to stay out of the spotlight of the UFO phenomena. This didn't mean; however, that I didn't keep in touch with the people I already made friends with. Nor did it mean I was no longer searching for answers.

About this time Sandra told me about a UFO conference in Tucson, Arizona. It was to be the first UFO Congress. I immediately decided to attend.

Another abductee I met at one of the abductee meetings I held, Cathy, was also going. We decided to share a room to offset the cost of the trip.

It wasn't long before we were on the plane to Arizona. I was excited to be attending in anticipation of the people I might meet who may have had similar experiences as me.

Hours later the plane landed and we went to the hotel to get settled in. I quickly unpacked and went downstairs to roam around and talk with people, telling some of them pieces of my story. It was then that I realized I was different from many of them. I seemed to have more memories of my Alien contacts and my thoughts were clearer on a number of facts. Most people seemed confused about what had actually happened during their experience.

I decided early on in the day that I would have to be careful about how much I said. I was still being cautious for a number of reasons, one of which was that for the past few months all my mail had come to my home damaged: in other words, opened. The person I was living with knew nothing about my experiences or what I was into and when he noticed the regularity of my damaged mail, he said he didn't want to know about it, so I never told him. I felt that opening up too much at the conference with strangers might not be a good idea considering past events.

I worked the conference rooms and spoke to many people. I then went into an art room and struck up a conversation with one of the artists by the name of Peter Clark. His work was amazing and I especially enjoyed the detail in his work. The large poster size picture of an Alien with big black eyes was what caught my attention. The artwork demanded attention and as I looked at it, it gave me the feeling the Alien was friendly. It was in the middle of a conversation with him that I felt a tap on my shoulder and a voice in my right ear. "I hear you have an interesting story. I would really like to hear about it sometime." As I turned to see who was speaking to me I took a breath of frustration. There he was, man number three! Just like Bill and John he had the same hair color and style, eye color, olive skin tone, glasses and, yes, you guessed it, those same beige pants. *Damn,* I thought, *will this never end?*

I told the man that I would talk with him some other time. For the next few hours he was always in my vicinity, watching, waiting, carrying a black backpack with him at all times.

Without speaking to him, I went up to the room at the end of the night to find Cathy already there, lying in bed. We had just begun to talk about our day when she brought up, what she called, "something peculiar" she had seen that day. "Miriam, have you seen the guy that has been around here today? He looks just like Bill! He has the same hair, glasses, skin!" She sat straight up in bed and said, "He even has the same beige pants!" I told her that I had seen him also and he approached me to talk with him: I was happy she saw him because up until that day I was the only one who had seen more than one of these men. I was ecstatic because it confirmed that I was seeing these men clearly. Both Cathy and I had many conversations about our disbelief over the similarities of these men.

Over the next five days this man followed me almost everywhere and we talked briefly on several occasions. I felt it was in my best interest to find out what I could about him. He told me during our conversations that he was a computer programmer—big surprise. He said he was writing a book on Alien technology and wanted to know what I knew about it, asking all the same type of questions that Bill and John had.

There were many people, complete strangers, who, over those five days, came to me and told me that I was being followed. Some of them were clearly concerned for my safety. I thanked them and told them I wasn't concerned. I had come to the conclusion that if these men meant me harm they would have done it by now.

Even stranger was that there were *two* of these guys at the conference. In both cases they had the same hair, glasses, skin tone, and yes, beige pants. They also carried *identical* black backpacks. The one that talked to me was taller. The short one would run every time I would get close to him. I guess he wasn't supposed to make contact with me in any way: at least, that's what I assumed.

During this time some of the people I met tried to get a picture of the short man for me. If he saw us he would leave and sometimes literally run away. In the end I did manage to get a decent picture of the tall, clone-like man and a profile picture of the shorter one. Comparing the photos, one would think they were twins, with the exception of their height.

At one point during the conference I had a long coffee with the tall clone. My intention was to try and find out as much as I could about him. I asked why he was so interested in the technology aspect of this phenomenon. He told me he was writing a book on the subject: *The ABCs of UFOs.* It made sense but I didn't trust him. Our conversation revolved around what I had been told by the Aliens. I gave him bits of information in an attempt to gather my own information from him. One thing he was adamant about was that I should *not* go to the Four Corners Area. He told me it was too early to go there and that I would not be able to accomplish what I needed to do. "It's not safe for you at this time," he said. I really had no idea what he meant but I felt as though he was warning me to stay away from there, at least for the time being. When I asked him to go into more detail as to why I should stay away he refused to be clear with his answer. He did, however, talk about the military presence in the area and the underground bases, both of which I was well aware of because the Aliens told me and showed me these when I was with them.

When I got back to Vancouver it was with guns loaded. Now I had ammunition for Bill and John since Cathy saw the "clones" in Tucson. I pressed Bill for answers and he finally did share some interesting insights. Apparently, at some point, he had been in the United States Military. He told me that he was part of a mind-altering program that took place in the 1970s. The program had deeply moved him, changing his life. It was one of the main reasons he got involved in the research of the UFO phenomenon. I sat in a restaurant with him while he told me tales of his time with the military and that he knew people that worked in the FBI and CIA. This didn't surprise me since I had highly suspected this for some time already.

At one point during our conversation Bill asked me how I meditated so I told him in some detail, step-by-step. "I only ever use white light," I said. "When I ground myself to Middle Earth I grab on to green crystals to hold me to the Earth." When I told him this he seemed surprised that I would do this.

"Have you been to the centre of the Earth?" he asked.

"I astral-traveled there with an Alien guide." He told me that he was surprised I saw Middle Earth as not many people have been there before. He said that he too saw the green crystals, only he implied it was in body, not spirit.

This in-depth conversation almost didn't take place. Before he opened up to me I told him that if he didn't start talking and being straight with me, I would leave and tell everyone that he was not to be trusted. It was our first real conversation—as well as one of the last.

My relationship with John was more established than with Bill, so when I approached him about my questions and concerns I thought I may get more information from him. At the time both he and Bill were taking a lot of trips to California and then on to Russia. He told me they were helping to put super-computers in place for a Russian government project. I demanded that he tell me how he knew as much as he did about UFOs and Aliens. He explained that everyone in his office was interested in them and that was where he got most of his information. I wasn't pleased with his lack of explanation and pressed him further.

As I had with Bill, I told John that unless he opened up with me I wouldn't speak to him again. John seemed to have an outrageous answer to every question including that all his information came from Bill. He told me about the government's technology that enabled them to listen to telephone conversations, listening for key words. If they heard any of these words they would automatically record the information to be assessed at a later date. He told me that the government of Russia and the USA had remote-viewing programs, which Bill was apparently involved with for a short time.

Not long after I confronted Bill and John, they slipped away into oblivion. No one ever heard from them again. After Cathy and I started talking to people about the men in Tucson I think they knew their cover was blown and they had to leave the UFO scene in Vancouver.

After the conference I sent a picture of the tall "clone" to a contact I made there. She in turn sent it to a friend of hers in another city in the USA who complained of being followed by a man with a similar profile. The woman was apparently shaken when she received the picture because the "clone" looked exactly like the man that was following her!

I tried to get a picture of Bill but was never successful in doing so. I did, however, have a couple of pictures of John from before the conference. When I compare the three different men in the pictures, I can see that they do have some striking similarities. The fact that they all have the same beige pants only adds to the bizarre intrigue.

Shortly after John and Bill disappeared I was back at work at a café job. One day I looked up and there he was—man number five. *Damn! Would it never end?* I treated him like any other customer at the counter while thinking, *He better not talk to me about anything other than the ordinary if he knows what's good for him!* He had the same hair color and style, eyes, glasses, skin tone and yes, those damn pair of beige pants.

I found out over the next few weeks that his name was Seth. He came in on a regular basis and always had a quick chat with me at the counter while he got his food. Our conversations were about mundane things like the weather. I did, however find out through our conversation that he worked for a computer company. They *all* worked for computer companies—who were these guys? I thought if they wanted to hurt me they would have done so already. I did my best not to let it bother me.

****

I wondered what it was that made me so important to have all the attention I had had over the past few years. I decided that it was in my best interest to step out of the UFO community completely and stop telling people my story. I felt that if I kept talking I may be in danger and I wouldn't be able to complete the mission I was given by the Aliens: to tell people who they were.

I broke off almost all contact with the people I had met in the UFO community. It was a decision that made me feel safe again. Slowly, all of the strange attention I was having slipped away and I was left to live my life.

Except for the presence of Seth. He stayed in my life and no matter where I was he seemed to find me. If I changed jobs or moved, it didn't matter. Every time I booked a flight to go anywhere for the following twelve years I would run into him, usually within three days. He would ask me if I had any trips planned and where I was going, what I would do when I got there, etcetera. It was normally a brief conversation; once we chatted for two or three minutes I wouldn't see him again until the next trip.

I drifted back into daily life as I tried to blend in. When the time to begin the work came, I would know, and so I let go of the UFO world in order to mesh with society again as I quietly waited…

ARIZONA SPIRALS

For twelve years I stayed out of the limelight after making a conscious decision to step away from anything and anyone who was involved with UFOs or Aliens in 1991. I woke up one morning knowing it was time to begin my work again for the Aliens. I always knew the day would come when I would get a message to return to work for them. That day arrived at the beginning of 2003.

The last time I was in Arizona was in 1991. I was there for the UFO conference in Tucson. I knew I would be traveling to the Four Corners Area at some point in my life but I stayed away until 2003 *partly* due to the warning from the clones at the conference. He told me I should wait a few years before traveling there. My interaction with him, as well as those with the other clones, made me heed his warning. I always knew that when, and if, the time was right I would know.

I woke up one morning in early January 2003 and began to think about going to Arizona and the Four Corners. Over and over I thought about what this area would hold for me. It began to creep into my every waking thought. Four months passed and every day the desire to travel to Arizona grew stronger.

The Aliens had given me a great deal of information regarding this area in 1988. One of the most crucial bits of information was that the Four Corners Area would be important to me as well as to others like myself in the End Times. It was there, I was told, that others like myself would gather. It would be "The Safe Lands" near the end. I decided I had to look past my fear and experience it for myself now.

I knew that in order to visit all the areas I wanted to, I would have to rent a car. I decided to camp along the way to make the trip less expensive. Both the camping and long driving would be a first for me, so I decided to ask a friend to come along. Most of my friends were either busy working, having babies, or didn't have money for a trip so I decided to ask a new friend, Carrie, if she might be interested. She was a great girl that I'd met through some mutual friends. Although she was in her early twenties and I in my late thirties, we bonded quickly. As she had been laid off from her secretarial job, I knew she was free to go on a vacation. I called her and asked if she might be interested in a ten-day camping tour of the Four Corners Area. She said it sounded great and the idea of me paying for the rental car made it all the more appealing to her.

I quickly found a great deal on plane tickets to Phoenix. Prior to paying for them I called Carrie and told her I wanted to share a story with her before she made a final decision. I was nervous at the thought of telling her about my UFO experiences but I knew it was important to do so. We decided to meet the next day to talk things over.

The following afternoon we met for coffee on Commercial Drive. We stepped outside the coffee shop onto the busy city street as I explained the importance of sharing my story with her before we left. I felt the need to be honest so if she felt at all uncomfortable, or thought I was nuts, she could opt out of the trip. I could see that the build-up to my story confused Carrie.

I asked her to please allow me to tell the whole story before she began asking me questions. We turned down a side street that had less cars and foot traffic. It was the perfect day to be out for a walk. The sun shone as we passed the old houses with flower gardens out front. It helped me to relax while I slowly explained why I wanted to make this journey to the Four Corners Area.

Sharing my story of Alien encounters for the first time with people always made me nervous. After only a few minutes Carrie interrupted me. "Miriam I don't think you're crazy at all! There is so much we don't know about this world. You're the first person I have met that said they've had Alien contact but that doesn't mean I don't believe you." I was so happy and somewhat surprised to hear her response. As we walked we talked about several subjects that were controversial, from conspiracies to Aliens. I was somewhat surprised by her knowledge because it was far greater than I expected. I ended our conversation by asking her to think about it over night before she made a final decision about traveling with me. She told me she didn't need to think about it but I insisted.

Carrie called early the next day to reconfirm that she was comfortable with everything I shared with her and then asked, "What day do you want to leave?" After I hung up the phone I paid for the flight to Phoenix.

I knew that something lay just around the corner. After 12 years of being out of the UFO community I knew this trip would be the first step back into the strange world of Aliens. I felt somewhat anxious knowing I was going to the area that was extremely important to them. They had said to me, *You will lead great numbers of people back to the Safe Lands.* It was time—time for me to see the area that was so closely tied to my role in the cosmic UFO community.

In the days prior to leaving I tried to stay focused on planning the journey. It was great being able to plan this type of trip with Carrie because we were both willing to accommodate each other's desired destinations. In the beginning I told Carrie that out of everything we did I had only two requests: we had to drive past a particular mountain, Shiprock, and we had to drive through Hopi Land in Arizona. Her requests were to go to Santa Fe in New Mexico and visit Meteor Crater. I knew that over ten days we would have no problem accommodating both our wishes.

Prior to leaving I felt I had to read some of my notes from my writing of 1988/89/90. I looked for any reference to a man named Harold. When I found them I read the passages in detail. The Aliens gave me specific information about this man, as well as details as to how and where I would meet him. I felt that if and when I did meet him it would be in one of two places: the Four Corners Area of Arizona or Peru. It had been years since I thought about the possibility of ever meeting him so I wanted to refresh my memory about the details of who I was looking for. I told no one before I left Vancouver of the remote possibility of this encounter with Harold.

Carrie and I were off to Phoenix the morning of May 18th. I was excited and nervous at the same time. I didn't share the apprehension I was feeling about our journey with Carrie. My life had intermingled with the Aliens for many years and now, after a long hiatus from them, I was heading straight back into their world.

Our plane arrived in Phoenix two hours late—the first change to our plan. As a result of being late the car we'd booked was given to someone else. Since it was a holiday weekend, nothing was available! Left with little choice, we took a taxi to a hotel for the night. We were told they would have a car available for us in the morning.

We had a slow start to our day because of the car delay. Finally, by mid-day, we were heading north to Sedona. After hours of ridiculous bumper-to-bumper traffic, the car reached the top of a crest and what we saw was amazing. It literally, took my breath away. For years I had heard stories of how spectacular the Sedona area was. Pictures could never have captured the mind-blowing deep red rock formations that lunged from the earth towards the sky. These massive structures dotted the drive into the area. We could easily see why Sedona would be considered an energy power point on the planet.

Our first stop was an information centre. After wandering around inside and picking up some pamphlets I spoke to a woman at the counter. I asked her where she would go if she was traveling in the area. I explained that we were looking for places that were not high-profile tourist areas. Her number one suggestion was a place called Mesa Verde. I was excited as she told us about the ancient cliff dwellings in the southwest corner of Colorado. After a brief conversation, Carrie and I decided it certainly was a place to put on our must-visit list. We left and headed back to the highway and the horrific traffic, trying to reach Flagstaff.

We camped in Flagstaff after pulling in late that night. Although we knew it got cold over night in the desert, we were still shocked at how cold it was as we shivered the whole night away. Early the next morning we crossed the desert on Route 180, heading east towards Albuquerque. Along the way we stopped to see The Painted Desert, Meteor Crater and the Petrified Forest. The Arizona desert began to fill our souls with a deep respect and love for the land. The area was rich with colour and mystery around every corner. We quickly understood that there were two kinds of people in the world: those that saw nothing but sand and cactus and those that saw the life and beauty. We were the latter.

It was about 5:00 pm when we crossed the Arizona border into New Mexico and stopped in Gallop for gas and water. Carrie went into the store for water while I waited in the car and looked over the map. When Carrie returned we talked about our driving route. It was clear that we didn't have enough time to see Mesa Verde and go to Santa Fe. We decided that we could see a city any old time but the history and mystery of the cliff dwellings would be a rare sight. When we resumed driving we took the famed Route 666. Carrie and I had a laugh about the number of the highway. We had been told they were renaming it in a couple of weeks. Maybe people didn't feel comfortable driving down a numbered route with a negative association.

I was so excited that I felt like a child waiting to open Christmas presents. Before we left Vancouver I had briefly told Carrie the story of Shiprock and the Aliens. Back in 1988, when I was taken, the Aliens had shown me an image of Shiprock. I was on the craft when they told me that one day I would travel to where it was. For a long time after my highway experience, I wondered how on Earth I would find this place. It wasn't until two years later, when a friend gave me a magazine from the Sedona area, that I learned its name. Before taking our trip to the Four Corners Area I did some research on Shiprock on the Internet. The information was limited but it did inform me that Shiprock was sacred to the Navajo people. It was Shiprock, the Navajo believe, that brought their people to the area and this world.

The sun was low on the horizon. Orange hues began to come to life against the desert sky. It was then that I first saw the outline of Shiprock in the distance. My breathing became erratic as we inched towards its form. There it was, exactly as I remembered. When we got close I stopped the car to look at the beautiful silhouette reaching for the sky in the otherwise flat desert. I felt excitement rising inside me as I saw the detail in crisp focus. There, in front of my eyes, I could see the three peaks jutting upward from behind the rather flat slope leading up one side. The emotional wave that hit me was so strong that I began to cry. *There it is!* I thought. *It is real and it looks exactly as it did when the Aliens showed it to me.* After I had time to calm down, Carrie and I took a few pictures and then jumped into the car to continue heading north towards Farmington.

Night crept over the desert as we drove in silence. It had been an extremely long day of driving and we were both exhausted. Since it was so late we decide it would be best if we got a cheap hotel for the night. I was grateful for the fatigue as it allowed me to get some sleep without thinking about Aliens, Shiprock or the endless possibilities of my fate.

Early the next morning we were excited to be on our way to the ancient cliff dwellings. The drive to Mesa Verde only took a couple of hours as we crossed from New Mexico into the state of Colorado. The green meadows were postcard-perfect through the mountainous area that led to our destination. I wondered at the beauty as we drove past rolling mountains, horses, old wooden fences and the grass meadows, which looked blue because of the tiny flowers that blanketed them. At the top of a ridge we stopped to take in the picturesque surroundings.

After crossing over into Colorado it was no time at all before Carrie, who was navigating, directed me to the turn off for Mesa Verde. We turned onto the steep, winding road leading to the cliff dwellings. As we crept up the side of the mountain we noticed it looked rather ominous. The trees were all dead black and withered, standing like statues. Under the trees the new growth stood only a few feet high. In some areas it was like looking into an ocean of purple wild thistle. It was beautiful and at the same time dark in its appearance. Later that day we were told there had been a forest fire there a few years prior. Fortunately the fire didn't make its way to the ancient cliff dwelling sites.

After reaching the top of the mountain we found a parking spot at the main tourist center. It was midday so the sun was at its peak. We walked across the street to the tourist office to book a tour of one of the ancient sites. Our trip was on such a tight schedule that we went straight for the booking desk. We found a short tour that suited our time constraints, bought tickets and grabbed a map. We were told that after the tour we would be able to visit another site where we would be free to walk around on our own.

Our guide took us on a short walk around one of the cliff dwelling sites. The red rock clay had been made into bricks to build the walls of the dwellings. It was an amazing privilege to stand so close to these buildings. As I touched the wall I wondered who had lived there, why they left and what their lives were like. I could feel the presence of the people who had lived there so long ago. Closing my eyes for a moment, I listened to the wind and tried to picture the faces of the people walking about the dwelling.

The guide then took us over to the Kiva. She explained that this had been a place where Earth Ceremonies were held by the people who had once lived there. Although the people were long gone I still somehow felt we were intruding in the private homes of people that had not invited us.

When the tour was over we decided to check out the free tour site at Spruce Tree Palace, another spectacularly large cliff dwelling site. When we arrived, we followed the other tourists on the footpath towards the site. We took a few pictures along the first part of the trail, then Carrie walked on ahead of me. She disappeared around the corner as the trail curved around in a U-shape. It was getting hotter and even in the shade the heat's effects were overwhelming. The trees' shade was cooling, so I took my time catching up to her.

I meandered around the corner of the trail. My head hung low from the overwhelming heat. As the trail curved around I lifted my head and looked up the slight hill where I saw a Native American man with short black hair looking at the cliff dwelling with another person. *Oh my God, it's Harold!* I shook my head and blinked. *Okay Miriam, it can't be him, it just can't! You're crazy and this is just going too far!*

A million thoughts flashed through my mind all at once. *What should I do?* I felt like fainting and screaming at the same time.

After I caught up with Carrie I briefly told her the story of Harold and the Alien connection. In 1988 the Aliens told me that one day I would meet a Native American man on top of a mountain. He would have short black hair and his name would be Harold. I would recognise him when I saw him. Apparently he would approach me when we met and he would teach me a great deal. I was in shock that the man I just laid eyes on could possibly be the man I had been waiting to meet for many years.

I wondered how I could confirm it was him, *How can I find out his name?* I thought. Then I remembered that, if it indeed was him, he would approach me. Carrie and I walked around the site, but I was completely distracted as my mind reeled from the possibility of meeting Harold.

Carrie kept telling me to go and talk to him but I felt I had to wait for him to approach me. We began walking back to the car on the trail, and I waited to see if the man would approach me. When we were about 20-feet away from him I noticed he looked at his companion and then began walking towards us. My breath felt like it stopped; my heart quickened and I swallowed hard. *This could be a defining moment in my life,* I thought as I felt the energy of it. I didn't look back. *What if it is Harold? What would it all mean? Why was I led to him? Why was I drawn to taking this trip to Mesa Verde? Why did the Aliens tell me about him?* I heard quick steps behind me and as I looked to my left there he was, walking alongside me.

"Hello," he said. I beamed and thought, *My God it must be him!* We began a conversation about the ancient site Carrie and I had just visited. He then told me his name: Harold! I felt like breaking into tears but I knew that I had to stay composed. I couldn't fathom what it all meant. *What, if anything, lay in the future for the two of us?* I wondered.

As we walked the trail heading back to our cars, Harold pointed to a side trail where we could look at an example of poison ivy. Neither Carrie nor I knew what it looked like so we veered off to have a look. The trail was only about 25-feet long. We all stood together at the end of the trail listening, while Harold showed us the leaves of ivy. He then began asking about our trip: where had we been and where were we going? We gave them a brief overview of our travel plans then told Harold and his friend that we were impressed to see the Navajo people still had very strong cultural roots. One of the most wonderful aspects of the trip was our introduction and exposure to the people and their culture.

Harold then told us a story about the wind in his native language. As I listened to him the most amazing image came to me. While looking into his eyes I saw spirals going back into them as far as I could see. They were never-ending. In that millisecond there was a flash, like a cover being raised from over his face. He no longer looked human; it was indescribable. It was so strange and fast that I barely had time to acknowledge the whole experience. My vision reverted back to normal as quickly as it had left. I was then more intrigued by my meeting with Harold than ever. After such an overload of emotions, my mind was blank as we all walked the trail back towards the parking lot.

When we reached the tourist office Harold and his friend gave us some advice on where to camp in Monument Valley. We said good-bye and Carrie and I headed back to our car. The farewell seemed too normal for such an abnormal afternoon! As the two of us walked on the sidewalk together I let my emotions run free as I cried and told Carrie details of what I just experienced.

Carrie thought I should tell Harold the story, but I could barely think clearly, let alone collect my thoughts enough to tell him! There was no way I could explain a lifetime story of Alien contact to this man in only a couple of minutes. Questions were swirling through my thoughts as I wondered what our encounter meant. This was a significant moment in my life and I needed time to assimilate what had happened and contemplate why it had happened.

"Miriam, he's coming!" said Carrie as we stood at the trunk of our car. Harold and his friend quickly caught up to us and asked if we wanted to go with them back to Cortez and hang out. I really wanted to go but, sadly, Carrie wasn't interested. She kept saying that we wouldn't have enough time to cover our planned areas of interest if we took a detour. After a short conversation with the men we exchanged email addresses and they left. The two of them walked away, got into a silver Jeep, and drove off.

This was all amazing but what does it mean? I thought. I shook with energy as I tried to hold back how much this meeting had affected me.

As we backed out of our parking spot, I had a feeling we would see them again part way down the mountain. Sure enough, they were there, parked on the side of the road. We waved as we passed them. *Why was I tuning in to this man?* I often had this happen with close friends but not with complete strangers. It only solidified my confirmation that we were indeed meant to meet.

Shortly after we left we realized we didn't know what route to take to Monument Valley. We pulled over at the next available rest area and looked over the map. There was only enough room for one car at the edge of the mountain. A moment later, we saw the guys again. This time they waved and passed us. After we were on our way again we noticed a vehicle that looked like Harold's pull in to a parking lot at the bottom of the mountain. We weren't sure who it was so we just kept going. When we didn't stop the vehicle kept driving straight through the parking lot and back onto the road. It followed directly behind us. We realized it was the two of them, so we stopped with our windows down. Harold pulled up and asked one more time if we wanted to go with them. We told them we couldn't, all the while wishing we could. I had to respect Carrie's wishes; however, I told him he would definitely be hearing from me and then we drove off.

That night we camped in Monument Valley at Gouldings Campground, an amazing site with red rock reaching towards the heavens. When we woke we realized the full beauty of the area. It was spectacular to watch the sunrise spill over the rock, changing its colour as each second passed.

Our next stop was Canyon de Chelly. The red rock mesas along the drive were spectacular! The sun's rays made the rust colours of the rock come alive before our eyes. The dry stark desert changed in an instant. Each moment, the sun's rays changed the colour of the red rock from light pink to rich rust red. If you were to sit and look at one area of red rock all day it would forever change colour with the direction of the sun. Each hour brings to life a completely new view.

Canyon de Chelly is on Navajo reserve land. The Navajo own the canyon land even though it is a National Park. They still live on the canyon floor, herding sheep, planting corn and leading a more traditional life. From the overlook sites you could see corn growing and sheep grazing. Although it appeared to be a hard life it looked like the way life should be lived: in harmony with the land, not against it. They hold the land as sacred.

From the moment we arrived at the canyon we were swept away by its beauty. It took no time for us to find out there was a campground at the top of the canyon. Shortly after we arrived the owner of the campground, Stevenson, came by to say hello. He was a very friendly Navajo man. Through our conversation we learned that he could take us on a guided tour around Spider Rock, one of the lookout points on the canyon floor. This thrilled Carrie and I, as we would have a very personal tour of a sacred place. Everything was perfect and I finally felt like I could relax a little.

There was still plenty of time in the day to take in the sights at the top of the canyon since the hike to the floor wouldn't begin until morning. We viewed the bottom of the canyon from designated overlook sites on the canyon rim. Words couldn't capture the amazing life of the canyon floor. The life in the canyon captivated us, not only as it appeared in the present, but also as it had once been in the past. We couldn't understand why there weren't more tourists because it was one of the most interesting and breathtaking sites we had seen on our trip so far. We were both thankful it still had its innocence. We watched the sunset at one of the lookout points and said good night to the spirit of the canyon.

7:00am came early as Carrie and I headed out with Stevenson and one other camper to hike to the canyon floor. We took lots of water with us. I was having trouble with the heat so Stevenson told me to walk slowly and I would be fine. He took us down the side of the canyon towards Spider Rock. The wind whispered to us as we walked and Stevenson recounted stories of his people. Along the way he showed us small cliff-dwellings and broken pottery shards. We didn't disturb anything out of respect and were grateful to Stevenson for sharing it all with us.

The heat was exhausting and I felt as though I wouldn't be able to hike back to camp. Luckily, there was a creek that ran along the canyon floor hidden by trees on both sides. We took a short break by lying in the cool water. Everyone laughed at me as I enjoyed the cool water running over my whole body. As I lay there, splashing the water on myself, I took a moment to step back in time. *How many before me found this refuge in the waters of the past?* I felt honoured to make a personal connection with the canyon floor. After hours of hiking we made our way back to the campsite. I took in every moment of our walk: the cool water of the creek, the red rock on the canyon walls and the green grass that covered the canyon floor.

When we finally arrived back at camp, Stevenson graciously invited us to have dinner with him. We accepted his offer and drove into Chinle to a restaurant. After our long hike and days of only camp food, the relaxation of being served dinner was wonderful.

When we got back from Chinle we saw a vehicle pull into the campground and choose a spot two sites over from us. We watched as they set up their tent and settled in. As usual, Stevenson made his way over to the couple to chat with them for a few minutes.

After Stevenson left, the couple walked over to our campsite to say hello and introduced themselves as Barbara and Zack. Our conversation consisted of the usual: Where have you been? Where are you going? What do you think of the area? Carrie and I were confused by the entire conversation. We both felt that they were lying about who they were and where they said they had been. Some of the information they gave us seemed unusual and we both had a bad feeling after talking with them.

Barb and Zack said they were married, but by the way they spoke it was as if they were making their story up as they went along. They told us they spent the day prior at the Grand Canyon, hiking to the bottom *and* back up in the same day. They explained how hot and tiring it was. That didn't make sense! Barbara was as white as a sheet with no tan at all anywhere—not even on her hands! If she had spent the whole day hiking in the canyon she would have colour *somewhere* on her body! Even sunscreen would not have been enough to keep the sun off. Secondly, we were told that if you hike into the canyon, you have to camp on the floor because you wouldn't make it back up before it got dark. The hike took about 8 hours one way. Carrie and I knew that something wasn't right about these two people, but we weren't sure what it was.

That night we were both exhausted and decided to go to sleep early. Neither one of us had been sleeping well since our camping trip began. Every night I would wake up at least two, or even three, times. I looked forward to the early night so I could possibly catch up on my sleep.

Waking early in the morning I opened my eyes and the moment I did I *knew* something was wrong. I felt extreme anger—for what reason I wasn't sure.

We crawled out of the tent and I told Carrie how I was feeling. I asked her to give me some time to myself so I could try to shake the awful feelings I was having. I couldn't remember ever feeling this way before. Not only was I angry but I felt exhausted as well, despite the fact that I had not awakened in the night. I was as tired as if I had run a marathon; I was drained of every ounce of energy.

Over the next 30 minutes we both got dressed and began to make breakfast without speaking. I then said, "I didn't wake up at all last night. I was completely *out*! So why do I feel like this? Maybe something happened last night." I began to look for cuts or marks on my arms, legs and stomach – anywhere I could see my own skin.

"You know Miriam, I didn't wake up last night either!" said Carrie. It became clear that we had both had a strange night. I was beginning to think that maybe I had been taken by the Aliens. Carrie and I looked over my body for any sign of being taken but found none.

Zack then came over to say good morning to us. After some small talk he asked, "Did you hear the strange whizzing sounds last night?"

"No," I replied. "What are you talking about?"

"Last night—I can't believe you didn't hear anything!" He went on to describe a sound that was like a shrill zzzzz that went from campsite to campsite before staying around our campsite for a long time. "It kept Barbara and I awake last night. We were so freaked out that we were going to go and find Stevenson to find out what was going on!" Hearing this, I began to panic. The possibility of a visitation the night before seemed more real with his news.

For the next half hour I walked around very upset by the events of the morning. I didn't want to talk with Barb and Zack anymore. The fact that they told me about the strange noises made me even more upset. *Why did I not remember? Did Aliens take me and why? Was it my imagination?* I left the questions unanswered for the time being in an attempt to keep my sanity.

That day Carrie and I were going to The Grand Canyon, passing through Hopi Land. I was excited about the layout of the day but I still felt tired and sick. I tried to shake off the morning's events, but found it hard to do so. We were packing up our gear, preparing to leave, when Barbara and Zack came by one more time. They gave us a pass to enter into the Grand Canyon—it would save us 25 dollars on the entrance fee, which was great. One stop they insisted we make was a place where they had had lunch. Zack repeated his directions once more and even wrote down the name of the place, Keams Canyon, so we wouldn't forget.

We had one stop to make before we left, coffee with Stevenson. Carrie and I drove the car over to the coffee shack, where Stevenson was waiting, and he jumped up to say good-bye. We told him how much his private tour had meant to us both and how much we loved the canyon.

Just then Barbara and Zack came by, again! They gave us a map of the Grand Canyon and told us about a good place to camp, insisting we use the site they indicated. By now Carrie and I were more suspicious of them than ever. We already knew we wouldn't camp where they had suggested but thanked them anyway. When we looked over the map we found that the site they directed us to was the most remote site out of the hundreds that were there. Right after they left Stevenson told us not to camp there— he too was very adamant. His normally quiet and soft-spoken nature was not present as he gave us this advice. Carrie and I felt that we should heed his warning. We left Canyon de Chelly that day with mixed emotions: sad to leave the canyon and happy to be on the road again.

Within ten minutes of leaving camp we saw a raven flying alongside our car. For the next few hours we saw it again and again in the distance, sitting on the side of the road. When we got close it would pick up and fly alongside our car until we passed. Both Carrie and I thought it might have been sent by Stevenson to keep us safe on our journey, it seemed to be with us all the way to the Grand Canyon.

It was midday when Carrie and I pulled off the highway at a sign that read, "Keams Canyon" where there was a small store, McGee's Indian Art. Inside they had Hopi jewellery, masks, books and Kachina dolls. Kachinas are the spirits for which the Hopi hold ceremonies. Each spirit has a specific costume and the dolls are carved from wood to represent the different spirits. I was thrilled to be there.

After careful consideration I decide to buy two books and an exceptional silver ring with a Hopi design. To my surprise the ring was not expensive at all and it had an authentic "Made by Hopi" stamp on the inside. The woman who was working behind the counter was very friendly and helped me pick out the books she thought would interest me. As she began cleaning the ring with a cloth, I asked her what the symbols meant. She told me they represented man and water. She then squinted, deciphering the symbols, looked up at me, and then back at the ring. "This symbol is a sacred feather; this is a very special ring!" She paused and looked again. "This is a very rare ring. It has a sacred feather on it—they normally don't make them with that symbol for the public. This is very special." I was thrilled and knew that it was meant for me, understanding that it was another sign, showing me how, somehow, everything fit together in this quest. The ring had been waiting for me to come and pick it up. I felt as though I was stepping into a new life as I took the ring and placed it on my finger. The Aliens had told me about my deep connection to the area; somehow I knew I was connected to these people. The ring spoke to that feeling.

Carrie went back out to the car when we had finished shopping, while I went to the store next door to grab a coffee. As I entered I saw a number of Hopi sitting in the restaurant. When I came out of the washroom I fixed myself the coffee, paid and turned to leave. I slowly walked out as I glanced around the entire room. Five Hopi men were watching me. For a millisecond their heads appeared hyper-extended on long necks, reaching out to me. They looked at me with wide eyes in which I saw spirals, just like I'd seen in Harold's eyes. Once again there was a flash before their appearance returned to normal. In that moment I knew who the Hopi people were. I understood why they had knowledge on UFOs and Aliens; many of my questions were answered. It was as though all the dots and lines suddenly fell into place. I understood more than ever before why I stood in Hopi Land that day. By the time I got to the door to leave I knew that I would be back to see the Hopi people. My fate and the fates of many were tied to them.

I knew that I had just been allowed to see the Hopi people for who they really were. It was clearer to me at that point than it had ever been that I was on a new path. I knew I was meant to have the special ring with the sacred feather on it. A new chapter began for my life: everything I had been told in 1988 by the Aliens was being confirmed for me on this journey. My work was about to begin.

When I got back to the car I shared what I had just experienced with Carrie. I was shaking and calm at the same time. My path was now clear to me, yet I felt nervous because of the clarity. Furthermore, the recurring spirals baffled me. Carrie and I agreed that when we got home we would have to see if we could find any clues to the spirals' meaning. The search for the truth, as always, was ever-expanding. I did know one thing however: the spirals were a message. *The answer must be just around the corner,* I thought, *in the past day I have had a great deal of confirmation and clarity.*

When we entered the Grand Canyon and showed the woman our ticket Carrie noticed the date. It had been purchased the day after the couple from Canyon de Chelly said they hiked down to the canyon floor. In fact it was dated the same day they arrived in Canyon de Chelly. This was proof to Carrie and I that we had been right about them: they had been lying about everything. The question was: why? After taking into account the strange night at the campsite, as well as their lies, we threw away every piece of paper they gave us. I didn't want any of their energy around. The whole encounter made me question why they encouraged us to stop at Keams Canyon in Hopi Land as they did.

Our last campsite was at The Grand Canyon. We chose the site Stevenson told us about, at the top of the canyon near the entrance to the park. As we set up, a raven landed next to our tent. We saw this as a good sign that we were being watched over. Before the sun went down we went to the lookout points. Both Carrie and I were disappointed in our experience at The Grand Canyon. The vastness certainly was a powerful vision to see in person; however, after spending time at Canyon de Chelly and feeling such a deep connection to the Earth there, we felt there was no comparing the two. The sun was low on the horizon and the red rock appeared pale and washed out, making the view appear less dramatic as well. It was obvious we were viewing the sites at the wrong time of day to see it at its best. Unfortunately, we were now close to the end of our trip and this would be our only opportunity to see it.

As we were getting ready to go to sleep that night Carrie couldn't get her watch to work properly: it wouldn't let her set the alarm. We had to get up early to get back to Phoenix for our flight home so we were a little concerned. I told Carrie not to worry, the raven would wake us up. It seemed to be watching over us and, if it truly was, it would help us in this matter.

The sun of a new day came early to our campsite and, right on time, the raven sang to wake us at the exact time we requested. It was a wonderful way to end our time in the Four Corners Area. We had a quick snack and quickly got on the road heading south, towards Phoenix and our flight home.

We were both feeling sad that our time with the desert had to come to an end. Our experiences there filled our souls with a peace that is indescribable. The Four Corners Area showed itself to us in many ways that we knew would remain in our hearts for a long time to come. On the surface, the Earth there appears stark and almost dead. If you allow yourself to open up, it will jump up to your eyes, ears and all your senses and speak to you. There you can talk to the Earth like nowhere else I have ever been. It is as if the earth can truly hear you and it then whispers back. We both understood why so many before us felt this part of the world was a power center.

Carrie and I reflected on the intriguing set of events that had occurred during our journey. We looked forward to heading home, so we could have a hot shower and sleep in a bed! We spent the last leg of our trip with visions of red rock dancing in our heads. It was a journey for both of us that sparked new paths towards the fulfillment of our dreams.

As the flight came to an end and we touched down in Vancouver my thoughts turned back to the spirals. The moment I got in my apartment I decided to see what information I could find on the internet that may explain their message. I looked for hours reading little pieces here and there, but didn't find anything that gave me insight into why I saw the spirals and how they pertained to me. I got frustrated and walked away from the computer, leaving it completely alone for a few days.

When I returned to my quest I was able to follow the trail of information straight to the Southwest Indians and the Hopi people.

When I took a short break from my search I called my friend Anna. I told her briefly about the incidents that had taken place on the trip. I told her about how I had met Harold and that the ETs had previously told me about him. "Oh my God!" she said. "I remember you telling me about him years ago!" She asked if I was sure it was Harold so I gave her all the details of how we met. She was taken aback by the whole incident. Anna looked forward to finding out what the spirals meant since she also thought they had to have significance. I hung up the phone and thought about how Anna had been there to support me from the very beginning of this experience. It meant a lot to me that she was still in my life after all I had been through.

The sun shone in my little window in the kitchen as I sat at my computer. I had some spare time so I decided to research the Hopi people and their culture. Maybe I would find something about what the spirals meant to them. As I skimmed the articles on differentwebsites I found myself straying from my focus to reading about the Hopi people. I came across the Hopi Prophecies and began to read them. I knew I had found the answer to the spirals mystery I was looking for.

I read the words slowly, one by one, and began to cry. *Why have I never seen this before!?* The Hopi Prophecies were some of the things the Aliens told me word for word! I couldn't believe it. I continued to read and found something they named the "Blue Star Prophecy." *Could it be?* I thought. I almost stopped breathing as I stared at the computer screen with tears slowing streaming down my cheeks.

As I read the Blue Star Prophecy I realized then that no matter what I did or where I went, my fate was sealed. I surrendered to this knowledge. I went over to my drawer and took out the necklace I had bought so many years before. I had worn it for 14 years, never taking it off unless I absolutely had to. The only reason it was in my drawer was because the chain was broken and I did not have the money to buy another one. With tears streaming from my eyes I took the necklace from the box. Gently I put it in my hand, closed my eyes and took a deep breath. As I exhaled I opened my eyes and counted: one, two, three—all the way to nine. Yes, nine points on it! The Blue Star Prophecy tells of a nine-pointed blue star that would appear in the sky just before the End Times as a warning for people to prepare.

This was the same necklace the Aliens had led me to buy in 1989. They had said it would be important to me and to many other people in the future.

The warnings they gave me were clear: *One day a star will appear in the sky for all of man to see, nothing or no one will be able to hide its presence from the world. It will be a sign to the people that the end is near and it is time to prepare.*

After the trip to Arizona, seeing Shiprock and finding Harold I was amazed. Now I knew who the Hopi people were and why they had been so important to me before I knew anything about them. I understood that what I had experienced in the past as well as today was not a figment of my imagination. My role in this cosmic and global experience was significant. Nothing could have been more clear—I must begin my work, the work they asked me to do long ago, to tell others of them and to begin the gathering.

HOPI MEDICINE MAN

Time passed very slowly after my last trip to Arizona. Since returning and finding the Hopi Prophecies, my emotional self had been screaming to go back to confirm what I finally realized was part of my destiny.

I left Vancouver on June 18th, 2004. Once I was on the plane I knew there was no turning back. I was determined to meet whatever was waiting for me head on. I sat quietly and reflected on the past 16 years of my life. So much had changed because of my experiences with the Aliens. Thoughts swept through me in flashes; the past, present and future rolled into one. I could no longer think on one level as the tenses of my life intermingled. More of the answers to my questions seemed closer now than ever before.

Since my last trip I kept in contact with Harold through email. I was vague in my correspondence but did tell him that my meeting him was foretold to me in 1988. I asked him if he would be interested in meeting with me if I came back to the area and he agreed that he would. I wondered if I was meant to spend any more time with him, or if his role in my life had been fulfilled in the desert last year. If I hadn't seen the spirals in Harold's eyes, it's possible I wouldn't have had the same reaction when I saw the Hopi men. Those moments set in motion a chain of events that lead me to my truth, my destiny and some of my answers.

The wheels of the plane touched the ground in Durango. My heart beat with excitement as the wait ended, I was back: back to the Four Corners Area, where I felt at home. I picked up my rental car and bags before calling Harold. We agreed to meet that evening to talk. I told him where I would be camping and he said he would come by to see me later.

The sun was hot and the day was perfect as I drove into Durango. When I reached the campsite I set up my tent and waited, and waited and waited. I kept telling myself to be calm when we met since I was feeling rather emotional. He was much later than I thought he would be. I finally saw him pull into the campsite. Jumping out of his jeep he seemed happy to see me but I could feel his apprehension as well; clearly he was unsure of my intentions. It was a slightly uncomfortable hello as we hugged each other before deciding on a place to have dinner.

As we drove back into Durango the conversation was really about nothing at all. It was the type of conversation that takes place when both parties don't really know what to say to each other. I kept telling myself to remain calm—I had to remain calm if I was to tell him my story. *Oh, where and how to begin?*

We ordered our meals and, as we waited, I began one of the hardest conversations of my life. From the moment I opened my mouth to speak I knew I did not have the courage to tell him about the Aliens. How could I tell him a story that began 16 years ago—a story that swept into my childhood and changed my life? Instead, I opted for the easier route. I would tell the story as though it came to me through visions and dreams. I thought this would be the best plan of action considering the time constraints.

As I recounted my tale, I found it difficult to hold back my emotional attachment to it. Sadly, I allowed my emotions to get the better of me. I could see my tears were making Harold uncomfortable. He began to bite his nails and looked at me blankly. He interrupted and said he often met people whom he affected in a way that made them think of life differently. It was at that moment I realized I wouldn't be able to fully express the story of my life. So, I told him everything I could without mentioning my Alien encounters. Considering he didn't know me at all, I was convinced that I had blown my chance to share with him the truth as to why I wanted to talk with him and there was nothing more to be done. We quickly ate our meals, paid the bill and he drove me back to my campsite.

After the sun went down I walked under the stars and wondered what this trip would bring to me. The first day proved to be intense yet anti-climatic, leaving me feeling more emotional than clear. My thoughts were jagged and disjointed, keeping me awake as I tossed and turned all night.

At five o'clock I looked at my watch after only a wink of sleep. I woke abruptly about an hour later to the sounds of people outside my tent. I looked at the time and realized I wouldn't be getting anymore sleep. My hour of rest would have to hold me until I got to my next destination,

Canyon de Chelly. I was exhausted but drove out of Durango towards my next adventure.

Hours later I rolled into the campground at the top of Canyon de Chelly, grateful to be there. I was completely exhausted from lack of sleep and my evening with Harold; all I wanted was to set up my tent and sleep. I didn't see Stevenson so I walked a few campsites over to see if the other campers knew where he was. The three people told me Stevenson had taken some hikers into the canyon and wouldn't be back for a few hours. I thanked them before going back to my site to get some rest. The day was very hot but I finally slept. When I woke and exited my tent Stevenson was strolling over to my campsite to say hello. He was very happy to see me and asked if I wanted to go to dinner with him. It was a nice gesture but I had to say no, since I was still very tired. He then asked if I would like to experience a Sweat Lodge the next day and I accepted. I was excited to have been asked and anticipated a wonderful experience.

I didn't go far from my campsite all day and spent my time in reflection and thoughts of "what if." *What if this is all real? What if I am meant to be here? What if I am important to the Hopi people? What if I am crazy?* I pondered the intensity of my life as I drifted off to sleep that night.

The next morning my thoughts turned to the events planned for that afternoon. I had never been to a Sweat Lodge and my knowledge was limited on the subject. What I did know was that it was a sacred spiritual experience. I felt that I was meant to arrive in time to have the opportunity to participate. If I had spent the day prior in Durango I wouldn't have been in Canyon de Chelly until the afternoon of the sweat—missing it completely.

I spent the early part of the day touring the canyon, absorbing the view at the overlook sites and enjoying the red rock. I found it has a calming effect as you watch its colour change. I headed back to my tent to have an early light lunch before the sweat. The heat was overwhelming so I tried to find shade under the juniper trees. Stevenson did his usual rounds of the campsites and eventually came by to chat with me. We sat together talking about what brought me back and I shared with him, as I had with Harold, my story of what led me back to the area. He told me he thought it was good that I was doing the sweat and filled me in on what to expect. Stevenson then had to go and get things ready so he said good-bye and left me to my attempts at staying cool in the summer sun of the desert.

An hour later everyone gathered around the fire where Stevenson was warming the rocks for the Sweat Lodge. The heat of the fire was overpowering as the wood sparked and the flames rose to announce themselves to the circle of waiting people. I thought that this would be a time to mentally prepare for the experience so I sat off to the side, quietly reflecting on my purpose there.

The Navajo Medicine Man arrived and spoke briefly to everyone before entering the lodge. We all followed, into the dense air of the lodge, finding our place around the earth pit that was filled with heated stones. My thoughts began to calm as soon as I entered.

I cleared my mind as the ceremony began in order to allow the present moment to be my sole focus. As I listened to the Medicine Man speak, my meditation and experience began. The chanting brought me closer to my feelings than I had been in a long time. I cried—a lot—releasing some of the apprehension and fear I was holding about my journey. The tears and the ceremony cleansed me.

The ceremony took place in stages and with the completion of each step I felt calmer and clearer. It was an experience that deeply touched my soul. I felt fortunate and honoured that I was able to participate in this event and I made that known to both the Medicine Man and Stevenson. I also told them that I understood the ceremony had been modified for non-Navajo participants. Had it been performed for the Navajo, it would have been different. All the same, I felt the Navajo chants and sweat deeply and was grateful for the experience.

The ceremony was sacred and we were asked to keep the experience to ourselves when we left the lodge. In respect to the Navajo I am not able to tell you in detail the events that took place. After we emerged from the lodge we proceeded to the next stage of the ceremony: dinner. It was my first taste of mutton—a traditional meal. I loved it, to my own surprise. As we all sat together, strangers to each other, we felt like a small family. There was a connection we had that was so clear you could almost see it in the air.

As the night grew dark we lit candles and enjoyed some tea that was made from flowers one of the participants had picked a few days earlier.

It was a perfect finish to the day's events. The conversation was light and playful as one by one everyone departed to their campsites to turn in for the night.

My thoughts re-focused on everything that had led me to the Four Corners Area yet again. I still was not sure when I would be leaving to go to Hopi Land, but I knew that when my spirit told me to go I would leave. Until that happened I would simply go with the flow and wait. I walked in contemplation back to my campsite, settling in to a good night's rest.

Morning came and I decided it was the day I would travel to Hopi Land. While I was making breakfast, Stevenson came over to say hello. He asked me what my plans were for the day and I told him that I would be leaving. He then asked me to join him for a coffee before I left. This was an invitation I later learned was not extended to all his campers. I observed that the people he asked to have coffee with were the ones he was interested in getting to know. Often they camped at his site to learn more about the Navajo culture. Stevenson was always willing to share his knowledge with people who were genuinely interested. After I packed up I drove to the check-in area and sat with Stevenson to chat and have a "spiritual coffee," as I called it.

Stevenson was quietly sitting at the small table outside. As I pulled up he quickly went to get my coffee so we could sit and talk. Always a friendly, joking man, I enjoyed my conversations with him. However, the visit was brief as I was eager to be back on the road. I waved to Stevenson from my car knowing, as I left, that I would probably be back to see him before I left the Southwest. I still had almost a week left on the trip. I loved the canyon so much I felt as though I was saying, "See you later" rather than "Good-bye."

I drove down the road into Chinle from the Canyon and felt strength in my thoughts and myself. The sweat from the day before helped me to be clearer, yet I still had many questions about my future—a future that I had attempted to turn my back on for a long time. Even as I pulled onto the highway leading to Hopi Land, I could feel that my entire life was about to change. As I drove I kept saying to myself, "It's too late now! I'm here, I've come this far and I have to keep going just a little further." Everything that was told and shown to me on that fateful day in 1988 was about to be confirmed.

I could feel my breath getting heavy during the last stretch of road before my destination. I knew what I had to do but I was beginning to feel fear again. My breath quickened, my eyes began to tear and with each inch that drew me nearer to my final destination the fear became more intense. "This, is it... this will hold the truth for me...my truth. Calm. Stay calm Miriam." I told myself, "You can't get emotional like you did with Harold!"

For the last few miles I felt the earth change. Suddenly it felt like I was going home, as though I had been away for far too long and I was stepping back into my rightful place on this planet. It was difficult for me to understand my feelings.

I pulled the car into a parking spot outside the store, McGee's Indian Art, where I had bought my Hopi ring, taking a very deep breath. *Now is the time,* I thought. *Now is the time to step into my destiny.*

I sat in the car for just a moment and tried to center myself before I went inside. I held my breath as I walked inside, I then saw the woman who sold me the ring the year before. No one was in the store except the two of us. *It was meant to be. This gives me the opportunity to talk with her.* I approached the woman whose name was Jennifer. I told her that I had been in the year before to buy a Hopi ring and a couple of books from her. I began a conversation by asking what other books she would recommend that might give me a better understanding of Hopi beliefs and culture.

As Jennifer led me over to the book section I began to open up to her. I shared with her rather quickly and emotionally the events that led me back to her and Hopi Land. I told her in the same manner that I had Harold and Stevenson: I explained that I had visions in 1988 in which I was told that the Four Corners Area was "The Safe Lands." I told her about how I knew the Hopi Prophecies before I read them, including the Blue Star Prophecy. Then I told her about my blue star necklace and how I came to have it and about the mountain and how it was shown to me in 1988. I also shared with her the story of the Creation Of Man as it was told to me in the 1988 abduction and how it was virtually the same as the Hopi Creation Story. I told her as much as I could in my limited time of a few minutes.

Jennifer told me she thought maybe I should talk to one of the elders. At that moment I knew I was exactly where I was supposed to be. That was why I had been so afraid. I had known she would direct me to the elders without me asking. She spoke to me with such questioning in her eyes yet, at the same time, she was calm. It was frightening. She said, "Maybe you are the one we have been waiting for. Maybe you are The White Pahanna." *I'm not sure about that,* I thought. I knew I was somehow important to the Hopi people, however. Not only this, they were important to me as well. The Aliens told me of a people who were from the last world and had been taken to this world. The Hopi were some of these people. That was why I recognized them when I saw them the year prior. The Aliens showed me a race of people who had been saved from the last world because they were the spiritual leaders and members of the past world.

As we walked over to the counter I felt a sense of relief as well as apprehension at the prospect of speaking to an elder. I had always known, even in UFO circles, that I somehow stood apart from others. I was told information in such great detail that still, to this day, it's difficult to share it fully with people. The fact that I was instructed to remember my encounter sets me apart from many physical abductees, putting me in a very small group of people. The Aliens gave me specific instructions, which was part of the reason I was standing exactly where I was at that moment.

There was a lot going on inside me as I stood at the counter with Jennifer. She gave me instructions on how to get to the house of the elder on one of the mesas. She drew me a small map, telling me he was not practicing his Medicine anymore and no on knew why. She directed me to him because she trusted him and apparently he knew a great deal. Jennifer also told me where her house was on the mesa in case he wasn't home. She said that she would be home later so I could stop by and tell her how it went.

I thanked her for talking with me and for the directions. She went on to reassure me it was okay if I just arrived at his front door, unannounced—he may even be expecting me, she said. So, with map in hand, I said good-bye to Jennifer. I walked to the car with thoughts of how I would convey what I knew to the Hopi man as well as how much I would share with him. The one thing that was very clear to me was that *I* must not bring up Aliens; *he* would have to begin that conversation. If he was not the correct person to speak with I would quickly know. In this way I would learn how much *he* knew about the Aliens.

My emotions were back in check as I rolled down the highway, on my way to the mesa and the Hopi man. My destiny—my life—was about to change and I knew it. This fact swelled inside of me as I got closer to my destination.

The road leading to the mesa took only a few minutes to negotiate. I was mindful of not being intrusive to the people in their homes. I was a complete stranger from so far away—what right did I have to be there? As I felt energy of the people, the Earth and the Wind, it was all somehow familiar to me, as though I already had an intimate knowledge of the area. I knew that although they may see me as a stranger, I was stepping into my long lost family's home.

Once on the mesa I had to stop and ask a Hopi woman where the Medicine Man's house was. She, in turn, looked at me with a great deal of suspicion. I told her that Jennifer directed me to his home and that she had given me a map which I pulled out of my pocket and showed her. Somewhat curious as to my business with Robert Smith, the woman tried to extract information from me, to no avail. Finally, she gave me simple directions to his home. It was only a couple of houses away so I left the car where it was and walked over. As I did everyone I passed kept a close eye on me without saying a word.

I approached the open doorway slowly and knocked gently on the frame. "Hello," I called out.

"Hello, come on in," a man hollered from within. I peered around the corner to see a man getting up from his chair walking towards me. I asked if he was Robert Smith. He seemed somewhat surprised to see me. When he asked what he could do for me, I told him that Jennifer had sent me to him. He told me that he wasn't doing his medicine anymore, so he wasn't sure what he could possibly do for me. I explained that Jennifer thought he would be the right person for me to speak with.

Robert at first seemed a little reluctant to speak to me, shaking his head, telling me didn't think he could possibly help me with anything I may be looking for. He offered me a seat, however, and some coffee, which I declined. I sat at the small table and began to tell my tale, again in the format of visions and dreams rather than Aliens.

My conversation with Robert was extremely intense. I relayed to him how, in 1988, an experience changed me to the core of my soul. I told him about my information that the Four Corners Area was "The Safe Lands." I explained my "vision" of Shiprock and how it became reality. I also told him about meeting Harold and the spirals in his eyes as well as those in the eyes of the Hopi men. I relayed the Story Of Creation and how I was told about the star that would appear in the sky just before the end to warn the people to prepare and that this matched the Hopi "Blue Star Prophecy." I continued with the story of my blue star necklace—how I came to have it and what I believe it represents. I explained to him how I read the Hopi Prophecies and understood them and knew something of them as well. I told him so much and was so overwhelmed and emotional that I sat and cried with him. I could hardly contain myself but I knew *he* had to be the one to bring up Aliens. If he didn't, he wasn't the right person to be talking with.

After some time, he looked at me and just asked bluntly, "Are you talking about Aliens?"

"Yes," I replied. "But I had to wait for you to bring it up."

"Okay, okay, now tell me the story," he said. I then began to give him the details of my Alien abduction on the highway and all the details of my Alien contacts as well as what I had been told.

After some time passed, an older Hopi woman came to him and he asked me to leave and come back in awhile. I quickly left them alone, telling him I would come back later. I went back to my car and had something to eat and drink as I wondered what I could do to pass my time. Jennifer had told me that if Robert wasn't there, I could go to her house where her children would be home. Since it was almost time for her to be home from work, I arrived at Jennifer's home and found some family members and Jennifer's two children playing outside. Just as with everyone else on the mesa, the children were curious about me. They told me I could wait, so I sat outside with them as they played. I was in complete awe of the entire experience.

The oldest girl seemed eager to talk with me. She was a bright girl with whom I felt comfortable. It was wonderful to listen to her as she told me stories about going to school and then, just as easily and quickly, spoke about Hopi beliefs. The things she spoke of were all deeply intertwined with Hopi culture, yet she asked *me* what I thought about them. I didn't ask her any questions as I thought that it would have been rude.

The girl, whose name was Debbie, began to speak in Hopi to her sister. Suddenly, from their foreign language, came a familiar word. They had spoken it in Hopi, but to my amazement I recognized it. I immediately knew it as one of the words the Aliens had spoken to me many times in the past.

Debbie continued playing in the afternoon sun, not knowing how much her words had affected me. I asked her what the word meant. She told me it meant "thank-you"—a woman saying thank-you in Hopi. I was stunned, as this word had always remained crystal clear in my mind since they used it to communicate with me in 1988. After Debbie told me what it meant I realized that the voice I heard speaking in this language at the time I wrote it down was female. *My God,* I thought, *how far will this take me? How much do I need to see, hear and know before I stop questioning everything, and simply believe?*

After sitting in the blazing sun for a short time I got very thirsty. I asked Debbie and her sister if they wanted to go to the store with me. They eagerly said yes and we walked over to a small shop on the mesa to purchase a drink. Once inside I began a conversation with a Hopi man during which I felt a strong urge to turn and look around the room.

What are you doing here? I heard in my mind. Standing at the counter with his head turned and looking straight at me was a Nordic Blond Alien! With one glance one could tell that he was not normal looking. He stood about 6' 5" and had broad shoulders. He was very athletically fit and wearing a t-shirt and blue jeans. His brilliant blue eyes seemed to swim around the room. His hair was true white and straight, falling to the middle of his neck, while his pale, almost transparent skin covered his well-defined cheekbones.

What do you mean what am I doing here? I snapped back at him through my mind.

Again he asked, *Why are you here?* He didn't take his brilliant blue eyes off me as he waited for an answer. I looked at all the Hopi in the room, Debbie, her sister, the Hopi man and the woman behind the counter. None of them paid any attention to this man with even a second glance. It was amazing to see this because he looked so strange and out of place.

I told him, *The same reason you're here, I am coming home!* I stared into his eyes. He then looked away to pay for his purchase. He did not respond and I felt the telepathic communication come to an end.

We left the Nordic at the counter while we walked out of the store. I asked Debbie if she had ever seen the blond man before. She skipped along and told me she hadn't. I decided not to press the subject any further as I looked back to see if he left the building behind us. I wanted to go back and talk to him but something told me that he was already gone. I knew the moment I was sent to the mesa that my life would never be the same. Seeing the Alien confirmed to me, once again, that the Aliens themselves had a great deal of interest in me as well as what I did. I decided not to tell Robert about this encounter—at least not at this time.

As the sun went down in the Arizona desert Debbie walked with me on my way back to Robert's. At his doorway Robert hollered for me to come in. He smiled wide as I walked back in and resumed my position at the table. He then asked me why I was there and I told him again that I felt it was the right time for me to be there. I told him how I woke up one day in the beginning of 2003 and knew that I had to begin my work again. As a result I was brought to the Hopi people. I shared with him the long set of events that had led me to Hopi Land and his people: from 1988 to the spirals in the eyes of the Hopi men the year prior. My intention was to eventually share everything the Aliens had told me with Robert and his people. The purpose of this trip, I said, was to find out if the Hopi did indeed know what I did.

Our conversation was very much one-sided—I talked and he listened. I went into detail about some things, but I knew it wasn't the time to be completely open with him about other things. Certain areas of information had to be shared with the Hopi people as a group, *if* they allowed me to speak with them. I felt I needed to ensure they would listen and accept what I had to say. So, I told Robert certain things to see how he would react.

During our conversation, Robert would shake his head and ask how I knew all the things I was telling him. "You're too young to know all of this," he told me. "It has taken me a lifetime to know what you're telling me here today." He asked me why I hadn't gone crazy. I told him I wasn't sure. Most of the people we each had met knew *part* of the story; often they couldn't handle it. Often their imaginations would take over, turning everything into Aliens, making them paranoid and delusional.

We talked about the differences in where and how the Aliens came to people. Again, he was surprised at my detail. Finally, he stopped me and said, "Do you know how long you have been here?"

"No," I replied as I smiled at him.

"You have been here for three hours and you haven't asked me a single question."

"I didn't realize that."

"Why haven't you?" he asked.

"What could I possibly ask you that I don't already have the answer to?"

He shook his head and said that it was all very strange. I asked him what he meant by that comment.

"I have had people come from every country on the planet from Russia, New Zealand, Australia, Africa, South America, Mexico and North America—but this is different."

"How?" I asked, even though I already knew that I was different.

"None of them knew as much as you do. They always ask questions."

Many of them were unable to handle the information they received. Some had gathered information from others and only thought they had the knowledge, but knowledge is not a gathering of facts—it is an understanding. You can be lead to information but it is up to you to let it become part of you and embrace it into your soul. Once you've done this you *know* what the difference is.

I agreed with him that many people could not process the knowledge and information well. I expressed to him that I thought a lot of people only think they understand because they have read or heard information from others but it's very different when you know it from the Aliens directly or have experienced it for yourself. Knowledge and the truth resonate differently and become unexplainable for some; others must find it for themselves—it can't be taught. All spiritual teachers can do is help people along the path, it's up to each person to find the truth for themselves.

After a long conversation with Robert I told him about the Aliens speaking to me in another language and that I had written out some of the words, years ago. I asked him to look at them to see if he recognized anything. This was the only question I asked him in our time together. He looked at the paper and glanced at me, shaking his head again. "Where did you get this?" he asked. I repeated how it came to me from the Aliens and how I somehow understood the language when they spoke it. He seemed shocked. There, on the paper, were *Hopi* words. He didn't recognize every word and thought some of them looked like they were in the Navajo language. The more I shared with him, the more excited Robert became.

He asked me over and over why I had arrived that day. Each time I replied that it was my spirit that had led me there.

Robert clearly wanted to know more but I felt it wasn't time to tell him everything: I did, however, share a great deal with him. As the evening progressed he told me I could stay in his home if I liked instead of camping for the night. I accepted his hospitality, understanding that this would give me more time to talk with him. I left his home for a short while to have some dinner and then returned to continue our conversation.

I never asked him outright but it was my understanding that the Hopi people were in the middle of ceremonies and I had arrived on the last day. After the ceremonies were complete there would be a feast with all the Hopi. Robert asked me to stay until after the ceremony was over. I told him I would think about it but I knew I couldn't—it wasn't time for me to stay. My purpose in being there was to confirm to me that the Hopi were who I thought they were and that they had the same knowledge as I.

We discussed why Robert was no longer doing his Medicine. I shared my thoughts on this and it became clear that I was there at this time to help him as much as he was to help me. We told each other that we would keep our conversation private. I have done so up to a point but I must admit I knew I couldn't hold back everything and I knew he couldn't either.

It was getting late when Robert asked if I could call the Aliens down. I told him I hadn't done it before. Maybe I could, but I wasn't sure. I felt that my presence might be enough to have them show themselves.

We waited until it was dark and then drove out to the highway to see if we could catch a glimpse of them. At first I felt a strange sense that we would be seeing them but it only lasted a few minutes when, all of a sudden, I heard a clear *No!* in my head. It was then I knew they wouldn't be out. Robert was nervous. I asked if he had ever seen them before. He said he hadn't and confirmed that he was indeed nervous which explained why the Aliens wouldn't show themselves. They did not want to frighten him.

We headed back to his home after looking at the stars for awhile against the inky darkness of the desert night. The desert sky is enchanting, like a lullaby in the wind. The stars entice me to keep looking and looking until I become lost in thought over the mystery of the universe itself.

We got back to Robert's home late, both of us in need of sleep. I knew I would have to be leaving in the morning, as he would be performing ceremonies. We sat to have a brief conversation and, as before, it became emotional as I told him how much it meant to me that he remembered everything from the past and the last world his people came from! I cried as I relayed to him how happy I was that the knowledge from long ago had not been lost by the Hopi people.

"I know that the Hopi have a specific role to play in the End Times. They are the Keepers of the Knowledge." Then I asked him if other Hopi knew all he did.

Robert told me, "There are others, but not many."

"That's good. As long as there are a few, it will be enough." I didn't really even know why I said that to him at that moment, it just popped out. Some of the last words I said to him were, "The reason I am here is to remember who I am."

As I said this, Robert looked at me with a very big smile and chuckled, "I know who you are!" I then told him one of my *biggest* secrets from that night with the Aliens.

"Shortly after my highway experience in 1988, a memory came to me. When I was four the Aliens took me. During that experience they gave me something, which I then buried. They told me one day I would know what it was for and that I would go back and find it." As I shared this with

Robert he sat looking at me, smiling.

Then he leaned over and gently said, "Go and get it."

We gave each other a hug. It was nice for both of us to know that we were not alone. As I drifted off to sleep I wondered what would happen next. Could I fulfill the requests made of me by the Aliens? Only time would tell.

The sun wasn't even up when I heard Robert stirring. I tried to sleep awhile longer since the day before was so draining both physically and mentally. It wasn't long before the sun filled Robert's home and it was time to get out of bed. I found him already awake, waiting for me. He asked if I could stay until the ceremony was done later that day. There would be lots of food, he said, and it would be nice to meet some of the Hopi people. Even as he asked I knew I wouldn't be staying, I felt it wasn't the right time. I politely told him that I would see how things went and that I would maybe return later that afternoon.

There was movement on the mesa again as people were waking up and walking about.

Those that saw us as we stepped out of Robert's home watched us closely, some speaking to Robert in Hopi. I was sure they were very curious since I had spent the night at his home. To those that asked why I was there he replied, "She is here to talk to me."

We had been invited to breakfast at one of his relative's home. When we entered the house there was food and coffee already set out on the table. All the children came to take a glimpse of me; the adults were polite but I could tell they wanted to know who I was and what I was doing there. The family asked me a few questions, such as where I was from—simple questions in an attempt to make small talk. Meanwhile, they spoke among themselves in Hopi about the feast that was taking place that day. They asked if I would stay for it and Robert kept saying it would be great if I did. I thanked them and said I would decide later that morning.

Breakfast came to an end and I thanked them for allowing me to join them. Robert and I rose from the table and walked back to his home.

We didn't have a lot of time since he needed to leave for the ceremonies in the Kiva. We said good-bye with a hug. It was strange how much I felt akin to this Hopi man that stood in front of me. It was as though I had found my family in these people—I did not want to leave, but I had to. I also knew I would return when the time was right. Robert walked me to the car. I waved as I drove away, watching him grow smaller in my rear-view mirror. The road off the mesa left me feeling sad and, I must admit, that I shed a few tears as I drove away.

As always the day was hot and the sun was strong. I was going to see the Slot Canyons in Page Arizona, purely for fun. I was emotionally drained from the last few days and I was looking forward to being in the main-stream flow of tourists where I wouldn't have to think of my spiritual self or Aliens. That didn't mean my mind was able to be completely free. It just meant that I could listen to the music blasting in the car and gently go over everything in my mind. There is something about being behind the wheel out on the highway that is invigorating and incredibly freeing.

I pulled into Page in the early afternoon and went straight to book a tour of the Slot Canyon. It was perfect timing as I was told my wait would only be about 15 minutes for the tour to begin. Truly, the Slot Canyon was a magnificent site, but, as with most tourist sites, it was extremely crowded. The canyon with its swirling red rock is ever-changing due to water and sand erosion. It looked like the ripples of sand that has been blown from the wind except it is in red rock, not sand. The colours change by the min-ute as the sun's position changes. The light of the sun moves through the slots above to create vibrant swirls of colour on the walls of the canyon. Red, pink, mauve and even purple colours become visible. It allowed me to forget my life for a moment and take in the tranquility of the space.

At about four in the afternoon I was flying down the highway towards Mon-ument Valley. I remembered from my trip with Carrie that the campground there had quite a view. When I arrived at Gouldings Campground, I had just enough time to take a quick shower before they closed. Then I set up my tent and had a bite to eat. I spent that evening reflecting on the past few days as well as my immediate future. Now that I had met with Harold and the Hopi both of my goals for this trip had been accomplished and I wondered where I should go next. I still had almost a week left and no real plans.

When the sun was completely gone and the night air was creeping in, I lit my candle on the picnic table and highlighted the day's events in my journal. I could see the stars beginning to twinkle in the night sky so I decided to lie on the picnic table and watch them for awhile. The later it gets, the more spectacular the view becomes, yet I was tired so I knew I would only enjoy it for a short time.

It was my first night after meeting Robert. I reflected on him the Aliens and my life as I watched the stars reveal themselves. Then, in the distance, I saw something. It looked like a very, very, very faint star moving across the sky. *Was that them? Could it be? It just couldn't! Maybe it is a satellite—that's it!* It was then that the faint light moving across the sky *changed directions* by about 35 degrees and then traveled in a straight line again until it disappeared. *That couldn't have been a satellite,* I thought. *Could it?*

I was so exhausted from the day I simply had to sleep. I looked straight ahead into the night sky and I asked the Aliens to do something. *If you are there, can I see you before I go to sleep?* A huge white streak shot overhead, disappearing as quickly as it appeared. I shook my head as I crawled into my tent. *I imagined the whole thing,* I told myself. *It was a satellite or meteor—that's all.*

The morning brought its own question: Where would I go that day? The best I could do was continue to follow my spirit. After a light breakfast I decided to go to the shop beside the showers to see if I could get any ideas. When I went into the store a lovely man helped me with my purchase. As I always do, I asked what he would recommend seeing that was not touristy. He was happy to help and pulled out a map to give me some directions. I left, excited to explore his suggestions.

The road was spectacular. Someone once said that once you've been to Monument Valley, you will recognize it on TV constantly as its beauty makes it a perfect backdrop for different shows and commercials. They were right. It's beautiful country and it really does speak to you as you travel along the passages and turns, huge rock formations jutting up from the otherwise flat desert floor. I stopped the car and got out to take in the view. I stood, reflecting on the year prior with Carrie. "Carrie says hello from her spirit to you," I said aloud to the land.

As I pulled back out onto the main highway I watched the rock change colour as the sun rose. I could see a large mesa on the left off in the distance. That was where I was heading—the road less traveled. *This is just what I was looking for,* I thought as I made my way to Bridges National Monument.

After a rather short distance I came to the road marker and turned towards the mesa. I was looking for another, less noticeable, turn-off that would take me to something called The Goosenecks. The man at Gouldings told me it was amazing and really a must-see. I drove slowly and carefully after the turn-off since I was in a rental car and it was a dirt road. After about 20 minutes of driving I arrived at a gravel parking lot. There were only two people there—wow! As I walked away from the car towards the edge of the lot I could see The Goosenecks—the winding Colorado River. There was a boat traveling the river. It was so far down from where I stood that it looked like a tiny toy boat. The river was carved deep into the flat earth as it curved around in a U-shape. It was a spectacular sight to see.

My next stop was at the end of a gravel road at the top of the mesa. It was switchbacks all the way to the top from which I could see the large expanse of the desert floor. I never met a single car on the road and it was invigorating to have driven to the top. At one point I stopped to take some pictures and I saw the tracks of a vehicle that actually had its tires go halfway over the edge! It would only have taken two more inches and I am sure that they would have gone over. I was glad I chose to make this drive.

I made another stop along my way to Bridges National Park. I was surprised to find a single man there. I was nervous as I got out of the car since I was in the middle of nowhere and alone. I quickly let that feeling go as the two of us walked to the edge together. We were both in shock that no one else was there. As I looked over the edge of the mesa I saw one of the most amazing views I had ever seen in my life. The entire expanse of the area lay before my eyes. We took pictures of each other with Monument Valley in the background as the most remarkable silence fell over the site. It was as though the winds stood silent for us as we enjoyed the view.

The day was gaining on me and I had to hit the road if I wanted to see Bridges. I seemed to be jumping from place to place as time whizzed by unchecked; before I knew it I was at Bridges National Monument in Utah. I have to admit, I drove past the lookouts with little interest, feeling somewhat disappointed after the last few views. It would have taken a lot to top them. As always it pays to ask advice from the locals!

I suddenly realized how tired I was and simply had to rest. I decided to sleep for an hour at one of the car pullouts. When I awoke I quickly decided to head back to Canyon de Chelly. It was calling me softly.

I drove feverishly back to the Canyon. The road and fatigue were setting in on me and once I arrived at Canyon de Chelly I quickly set up my tent and got some rest. The remainder of the day was uneventful and relaxing. I spent some time with Stevenson and some time in reflection.

Night set in and the stars came out in all their glory. I looked up to see what clearly looked like a child's dot-to-dot—the kind in which you connect the dots with a line, the order being very logical. The formation of the letter C was in the sky, with one dot missing. The missing spot was the second dot at the bottom of the formation. Each dot was very bright. *Is that you?* I wondered. *How can it be? Really, it's just bright stars.*

It was then that I spotted a speck moving across the sky, much like the night before. The speck was so far off that if I blinked I had to really search for it again. As I watched, it seemed to head for the missing dot in the big C formation. Sure enough, it curved and went right into position where it *stopped* to complete the C formation. It then got very bright, just like the rest of them! They were like guide lights in the night sky. After it paused and brightened, it dimmed and began to move again in a straight line before turning about 40 degrees and heading straight again. It then passed over the corner star of the dipper. Then, it came back and positioned itself directly over that star, becoming extremely bright like it had in the C formation. It then dimmed to almost nothing and zipped off out of sight.

My God, doesn't anyone ever see this? I asked myself.

No one usually bothers to look, said a booming voice in my mind. I shook my head. I was so excited by what I saw *and* by the voice in my mind that I just had to go and find a phone in Chinle and tell my friends. I jumped in my car and raced to the nearest telephone. I called my good friend Dan and told him all about my last few nights in the desert. After talking for a short time I realized how late it was and decided it was time for me to get some sleep.

Once again I found myself asking the question, *Who am I?* There had to be a reason why everything was happening to me. Why did the Aliens keep such close tabs on me? I knew that what I had seen that night and the night before were the Aliens—I couldn't question it any longer. After I had met with a Hopi Elder and spoken of things that his people hold sacred and do not share with the public, there was no doubt in my mind that I was special in some way. The Elder only spoke to me because I had been led to him and his people. He knew this and so did I. I felt as though the display that night was a way to confirm that it was real. It was a validation of all that had come before.

It took quite awhile for me to fall sleep because of all that was on my mind. Finally, I drifted off. The top of my tent had no cover on it so I could see the moonlight when I woke up in the middle of the night. I could hear what sounded like dogs sniffing around outside of my tent. I was nervous and didn't want to open my eyes. I made a shush sound to scare them off and I fell asleep *immediately*—very unusual for me. I woke one more time that night to the same sounds before I fell asleep a second time.

As per usual at this campsite I woke to the sounds of flute music at 7:00 am. Stevenson always played the music of the Navajo in the morning. It was a beautiful way to be roused for the new day even though I was very tired since the dogs had bothered me throughout the night. As I stepped out of my tent, the heat of the day overwhelmed me.

When I went to take down my tent that morning I made a strange discovery. At the back of the tent in the soft, red, sand-like soil, were two straight lines. They started at the tent and went straight out about two-and-a-half feet and were exactly parallel and exactly the same length. The day before when I put up the tent I walked around the tent a number of times and these lines were not there. In fact my footprints were *under* the lines! I thought of the dogs, but could not think of how they would make these perfect marks in the soil. I looked inside my tent to see exactly where my head would have been and compared this to the outside. I was baffled: my sleeping bag hadn't been moved so I could see that the lines had been made on either side of my head.

I thought of the dogs again, remembering that they had been sniffing at my head outside my tent twice in the night. It felt like they had been right beside my ears. Why, then, were there no dog tracks where these lines were? None of this made any sense. When I tried to put all of it together I knew that something wasn't right. Was it just dogs? Was it the Aliens? Who knows? What I do know is it was worth questioning because the facts laid out didn't make any sense

I was restless and wanted to leave. Stevenson came by for his usual hello in the morning. I told him I felt like packing up and moving on. I didn't know where I was going, but I knew I had to leave. Stevenson suggested I take Highway 13 across the mountain if I was going back to Durango. He said it was a beautiful drive, which had an amazing view of Shiprock at the top. *Now that,* I thought, *was something worth seeing.* I looked forward to having another opportunity to see Shiprock.

Once I decided to leave, it felt like I had no time to waste. I said my good-byes to everyone, including Stevenson, and then drove off. Stevenson was right, the mountain drive was magical. Along it there were mesas all lined-up in a row, standing like soldiers against the backdrop of blue sky. It was spectacular! The beginning of the drive had some of the reddest rock I had ever seen, other than the red rock in Sedona. Once I began to ascend, the scenery changed and I saw meadows and trees rich with invitation. I wanted to stop and walk through them but never felt comfortable with that idea at any point. There were too many places for the car to get stuck, and often there were other people about.

At the top of the mountain there was an extraordinary view of the valley below. There was a light purple mist that covered the whole area. It was like nothing I had ever seen before. After enjoying the view, along with the butterflies and bumblebees on the thistles, I continued on my way.

On the valley floor I came across a gas station and trading post. It was more like a general store with seats outside so I bought an ice cream and sat to contemplate my next move. Navajo people wandered in and out. Some smiled at me in questioning politeness, while others looked at me as though I should not have been there. This was not a tourist stop and in my half hour there I saw no other tourists.

I sat quietly, enjoying the moment, when a Navajo man approached me. He was middle-aged and seemed nice enough. He asked if he could sit with me. I accepted, as I always love a good conversation with local people. We sat for a short time, talking about where we were going and what we were doing that afternoon. He asked if I would like to go on a hike with him. He said he would show me some red rock that was breathtaking. I felt I could trust him and, before I knew it, I was following him back across the mountain from which I had just come.

Once on the other side of the mountain, the small white truck he was driving pulled over onto the side of the road and I pulled in behind him. I followed him out of his vehicle and we walked over to a small opening in a fence. For a moment I thought I was crazy to be going into the backcountry with a stranger but that feeling didn't stay with me. The rock here was some of the most vibrant I had seen and I was happy to be walking alongside it.

Our walk was peaceful and I enjoyed the stories the man told me about his youth when he was a sheep herder. He did most of the talking as I listened. He spoke about the struggle between trying to have a traditional Navajo life while living in a progressive world. There seemed to be a great deal of pain in his story. I could clearly hear that it was his struggle as well as the struggle of his people. It was fascinating to have this rather intimate conversation and I felt privileged to be a part of it. I found it touching that this stranger, this man, was asking my opinion on such matters. He told me he was searching to find his own answers.

We walked a short distance and then sat to rest and talk. It was a beautiful moment of sharing and connection with the Navajo man. The day passed quickly and it was soon time to leave. He had a sheep to find and I had to drive back across the mountain to yet another unknown destination.

On my first trip across the mountain I had a feeling that I would receive a gift from someone. I pondered this only briefly because I didn't think I would be seeing anyone. Before we departed the man walked over to a pinion pine and tore off part of a branch. He explained that it was sacred to his people and told me how the pine was to be dried and burned to cleanse my home and my self. Often, he said, it was used in his people's ceremonies. The very act of him giving it to me was a very special gift. I knew about the pine and did want some but I would not take any on my own, nor would I ask for it. Such a thing would not have been spiritually right. If I were meant to have any it would have to be given to me. I was grateful to be honoured in such a way.

As with many moments on this trip I felt my spirit had led me to this moment so that the two of us could share our thoughts. I gave the man a hug and thanked him for everything. I knew that we met for a reason and also that I would probably never see him again. He quickly got in his truck and sped off.

I sat in the car for a moment before driving back over the mountain for the last time. The memory of the lights in the sky began to overload my mind again. I knew that each second I was in this area of the Four Corners was bringing me closer to my destiny. I could no longer push away what had taken over every aspect of my life; I could no longer deny what I was experiencing. It was time to begin the work They had asked me to do so long ago. It was time to start telling others my story and attempt to share my knowledge of the Aliens with anyone who would listen.

The light was waning when I realized that there wasn't a campground in the vicinity. I decided to continue to Cortez in Colorado. I had already been tired when I started my day and, as the hours passed, I became increasingly sleepy. Even so, my mind operated on overtime, thinking about the past couple of days: the meeting with Robert, the lights in the sky two nights in a row, the strange lines that appeared outside my tent. These incidents revolved in my mind and mixed with the past 16 years of UFO experiences. I also thought about the suppressed memories that re-emerged in 1988 after my encounter. I felt that the numerous moments on this trip were fitting everything together like jigsaw pieces, creating an undeniable picture. The small questions or doubts that I had held were all being wiped away.

I rolled into Cortez after dark and decided to get a room for the night. There was just no way that I could have kept driving safely. I bunny-hopped down the main highway through the town, stopping at motels to check price and availability. After the third try I found a room that was within my price range.

After my day of heavy contemplation I was looking forward to watching some mindless television to take my mind off past events. I got my things out of the car and took them into the room. Just then I noticed a man in a red car pull into a parking spot. He was also unloading and getting settled into his room. When I left to go for dinner, I noticed the man was still busying himself outside.

The walk back to the motel after dinner was short but I enjoyed the bustle of cars as it took my mind to a more casual place. When I returned the lot of the motel was filled with cars and the No Vacancy sign was up. Once again I noticed the man was outside by his car with the door to his room wide open. He looked at me as I passed him but we didn't speak.

I made a couple of calls and was about to put my head to my pillow. As I always do when traveling alone, I took safety precautions before going to sleep. The room was small but it had windows in the front and the back so I went to check they were secure. I found that the main window didn't lock. As it would take nothing at all to open it, I tried to call the office but there was no answer. I walked over to see if anyone was in the office, only to find they were gone. I knew I couldn't sleep knowing anyone could easily come in the window.

As I walked back to my room, once again, I saw the man at the trunk of his car. I went to my car to look and see if I could find something with which to block the window. I knew that if I didn't resolve the situation my motel room would not be where I would be sleeping that night. There was not much left to lose so I walked over to the man and asked him for his help. The moment he opened his mouth to speak I had a very clear flash: *This man works for the military and* maybe *he is here because of me.* He introduced himself as Gordon and said he was more than happy to help me. He suggested I use my tent pole to block the window—sure enough, it worked perfectly. We said good night and went our separate ways.

I was exhausted but decided to make a call to Janice before going to sleep. I wanted to share the story of the lights in the sky with her before I went to bed. I also wanted to tell her about Gordon and the military vibe I got from him. I had only been in my room for 5 minutes when there was a knock on the door. I put the phone down to answer it. Just as I thought, it was Gordon. He asked me if I was interested in going for a drink with him. I knew my impression of him was bang on and decided to find out who he was and what he wanted with me. I told him I would meet him at his room and we could go from there. On the phone I told my sister as much as I knew about this guy. I told her he drove a red car, his plate number, his hotel room number and the name he gave me. She asked, "Why are you going with him if you think he works for the Government? Do you really think that is such a good idea?"

"I want to know why he is here and talking with him is the best way to find out. I know that if he meant me any harm he wouldn't be trying to talk with me. Maybe I can learn something from him, you never know." I told Janice not to worry, I would be just fine and hung up the phone.

My body was tired and wanted nothing more than to sleep but I knew I had to find out who this man was and why he was there. Considering I had just been privy to a very large display put on by my friends the night before, I decided it might be worthwhile to follow through and find out what I could about this man. I did question my intuition, however. Maybe I was just being paranoid, but then again, it was a strong impression! From just looking at Gordon, I would have never assumed he was in the military—he was an older man with long, messy red hair.

I got to Gordon's room to find the door open. He was watching TV and jumped up right away when he saw me. He told me there was a pub a short distance away and asked if that sounded all right. I agreed and we took the few steps towards his car. We would have to drive there and Gordon asked, "Do you want to see my ID before we go anywhere?"

"It's okay, I don't need to see it." I told him.

His reply was very interesting. "Really? Are you sure? I know you like to do that: it makes you feel more comfortable."

I smiled at this strange man as I thought, *You jerk! What do you want from me!?* His comment confirmed all my suspicions of him right then and there. I have rules for myself, before going off with strangers there are clear steps that must be taken. My rule is to see their ID and call a friend or family member with their information, with the person's consent of course. If anything were ever to happen to me, the police would have a place to start looking at least. People with bad intentions usually steer clear after this request—or at least they stay in line.

We arrived at the pub and found a seat at a large, comfortable booth. I knew I couldn't leave my drink for even a split-second and I had to stay guarded during our time together. This included shielding myself so that if he too was gifted with any ESP, he couldn't see inside me without asking. The conversation we had was casual, but he really seemed interested in me asking where I was from and where I was going. The questions were normal but he really pushed when I avoided giving details.

The conversation that Gordon and I had was casual to start. We talked about our trips and where we had been. I would say that Gordon's interest in my trip was somewhat pronounced. He wanted details, and he kept approaching the subject over and over from different directions. I talked about what I did for work and still he went back to my trip. He talked to me about my car and the fact that it was a rental. He asked me if I knew that rentals have GPS tracking devices on them so that the company would know if I went out of state. He went into some detail about it. Then he told me that he didn't know much about it but some of his friends did and had told him.

Because of the vibe I was picking up and his talk about GPS tracking devices, I asked him what he did for work. Most people talk about what they do for work right away but he had made no mention of what he did, even after I talked about my work. This was not a normal conversation and, to me, it implied that he was trying to cover something up. When I asked him what he did for work, he said he didn't want to talk about it, telling me it wasn't important. After I asked a couple more times, I told him that it was strange for him to not say anything about what he did and that was it clear to me he was hiding something.

After a long, deep sigh he said, "First, I have to tell you that I am a civilian." *Right, no civilian says they are a civilian as an opening line!* He continued by telling me, "I do contract work for the U.S. military." After some prodding I managed to get him to tell me a little bit about what he did for the military. His work revolved around space technologies.

This was not a shock to me; on the contrary, I was only slightly surprised that this man was actually telling me this straight out. *Was sitting here with this man really a coincidence? Was I being followed? Was I just overwhelmed?* The only thing I knew for sure was my first impression of Gordon: he worked for the military and he had been sent to check up on me. He confirmed the first part. Why, then, would I question the second part of my initial impression?

I knew as I sat with this man some people would wonder why on Earth I would even talk with him. My reasoning was clear in my mind. If he was sent to talk to me and then I didn't talk with him someone else would be sent. Maybe next time I wouldn't catch them so easily. I knew I wasn't going to get any more information from him and decided it was time for me to go back to the motel to sleep.

When we arrived back at the motel, he was still telling me how much he would like to hear more about the trip I was on and how fascinating it sounded. I told Gordon that I was tired and needed to sleep and off I went.

I slept fairly well and woke the next day to the voices of people packing up their cars to leave. I looked out the window and saw a note on my car window so I went out to retrieve it. As I opened the door I saw Gordon at his car trunk—again. I went to my car to get the note to read. Gordon walked over. The note was from him, asking me to go for a coffee before I left. Almost immediately, he began asking me to share with him more about my trip. I politely declined but told him we could stay in contact via email. Again, I knew people would wonder why on Earth I did it. My reasoning was simple: keep your friends close and your enemies closer.

I left the parking lot of the motel wondering what lay ahead for me. I had four days left and it seemed that every day contained an event that touched me deeply. This trip was one of the most spiritual experiences of my life and it didn't seem to have an end to its intensity. I had no idea where exactly I was going. The car was pointing in the direction of Durango and so I kept driving.

It was a short time later when I pulled the car into an Internet café in Durango. I went in and sent some emails to friends and looked for new places to visit. While I was there I saw two guys sitting at a table with a map, speaking French. Before I left I asked if they were trying to plan a sightseeing tour. As a fellow traveler, I was also interested to hear where they had been. They told me they had traveled from Québec and were on their way to Mexico for a couple of months.

I shared some of my travel stories of Canyon de Chelly and then told them since they were so close they just had to see Mesa Verde. I also told them about the campsite at the top of the mountain there. It was nice to see some fellow Canadians but it was time for me to hit the road again.

On my way into Durango from Cortez I noticed a number of signs for campgrounds. I decided to go back in that direction to see if one of them would be a suitable home for the night. Once I went past a few signs I turned around and drove back towards Durango again. It was strange. I went back and forth on the highway a few times, undecided. Finally I said out loud, "Okay, if you want me to be somewhere, show me." I wanted my spirit to guide me to where I needed to be.

I kept my eyes as well as my senses open. My path became clear to me quickly. Three times I felt a pull towards one particular campground as I drove past it, this time I pulled in. Once there, I was happy to see that it had clean showers, a bathroom and a pool! Best of all it had a beautiful little creek that I could camp beside.

As I set up my tent I felt pleased with my location. I felt as though I could relax for the night, catch up on my journal writing and maybe even get some sleep. The day was relaxing and completely boring—just as I had hoped it would be.

When it was time for me to get myself organized for bed I made a trip to the bathroom. As I was brushing my teeth a woman and her child came in. They were the people from the campsite next to mine, which was only a few feet from where I had my tent set up. I am usually very talkative but I hadn't felt like engaging in conversation during the day.

I really liked the vibe I got from the mom. There was something different about her that made me stop and pay attention. I glanced at the girl and immediately saw a glimmer in her that I knew and understood. She would be one of the children that would be helped in the future by the Aliens—if and when that time came. She was one of the chosen!

This little girl was worthy of more than a simple hello to the mother. As always I began the conversation with this stranger with ease. She introduced herself as Kathleen Anderson and her daughter as Savannah. We had a great connection and I quickly turned the conversation around to her daughter. My observation of the child was that she was very intelligent, pretty, and yes, gifted in intuition. I wanted to get a feel of whether or not this woman had any idea of how special her child was.

Our conversation went on long enough for us both to be finished our business in the bathroom and we all left together. Her husband was outside in the darkness waiting. He introduced himself as Jason. Again I got a strong vibe that I was meant to meet these people. They were a special family for some reason—a reason that even I could not explain. I kept talking with them trying to get a sense of why they were in the Four Corners Area. It didn't take long to find out they were looking into the possibility of buying land in the vicinity.

I shared with them some details of my travels to the Hopi and Navajo lands. I also expressed to them how special I felt the Four Corners Area was. It was a fascinating conversation between the three of us. Savannah was getting restless as we all walked back to our sites and she needed to be put to bed.

Kathleen went ahead to settle Savannah in for the night, leaving Jason and I to talk in the darkness. As always I looked for the stars, but the clouds were out that night and there were none to be seen.

Our conversation became very intense. He shared with me that they had become discouraged in their search for a piece of property to buy in the area. Just that day they had asked for a sign that they were doing the right thing buying land in the area. When he said that I knew I had to let them know they were exactly where they were supposed to be and that they should keep looking.

I tried to tell Jason how I came to be in the Four Corners Area. I began in my usual way, using the guise of visions and dreams. I shared with him that I was told the Four Corners Area was the "Safe Lands" in the "End Times" and that I had been shown Shiprock and that I was drawn to the Hopi people. I told him as much as I possibly could during our brief conversation. I was happy that I met them and strongly encouraged him to keep looking for land. I told Jason I thought they were meant to be there and to not give up.

Time, as always, had gone by very quickly and we both needed to get some sleep. I gave Jason a big hug and told him how wonderful it was to meet him and his family. He then asked me to please come by in the morning to have a coffee with them before I left. As Jason walked away I took one last look up but still there were no stars to be seen. *It will be quiet for me now*, I thought as I settled into my tent.

Morning came early as it always does when you're camping. As soon as I got out of my tent I began packing my things to leave. I could see the Anderson family was awake and having breakfast at the next site. I kept my head down and focused on my packing. I would go and see them after I finished my task at hand. It only took a couple of minutes before Kathleen came rushing over to me. She was excited to see me again and told me I just couldn't leave without having a coffee with them. She told me that my conversation with her husband the night prior had affected him deeply. I knew I would be going over but I guess they saw me packing and thought I was running off, which was never my intention. I agreed to her request and reassured her I wouldn't leave until we had time to visit.

After the car was packed and ready to go I walked the few short steps over to the Andersons'. I was greeted with a great deal of excitement and proud smiles as I was introduced to Jason's mother Patricia. I liked her right away. After only a few minutes my feelings were reaffirmed—they were exceptional people. I was happy to have been asked to their campsite.

The four of us sat beside the stream having an intense conversation while Savannah ran around, playing. She had striking blue eyes that spoke without saying a word. Every once in awhile she would come over and ask a question. I think she was just as intrigued with me as her parents were. I couldn't convey to them at the time that I was just as intrigued by them.

Kathleen told me again how much the conversation between Jason and I had affected him. She asked if I would be willing to share the story with her and Patricia. I was more than happy to do so since I felt it was important that they buy land in that area. As I spoke with Kathleen and Patricia they slowly opened up to me as well.

I found out what led them to their decision to buy land and become self-sufficient. I told them I was pleased they were doing so. As we shared our stories I began to get flashes of images and thoughts about each of the Andersons; I shared my visions and this deeply touched each of them, moving them to tears. It was an unforgettable experience for us all.

I could clearly see that we were meant to meet for reasons that even I may not fully understand. They asked for confirmation that they were doing the right thing in looking for land in the Durango area the day before I arrived. My arrival most certainly was that confirmation for them.

I tried to convey my experiences to the Anderson family in such a way that they could understand and accept it while making sure the message was crystal clear. I could have sat with these people all day but I knew I had to get on the road again. If I stayed, my presence might have been downplayed and I didn't want that to happen. We exchanged email addresses so we could keep in touch. After we all hugged and said our good-byes they still asked me to stay once again, but I knew it was time to leave.

I walked away from that campsite knowing full well how much of an effect I had on these people. I jumped in my rental car and began to slowly drive off. Again I found myself wandering through my past, present and future which seemed to be rolling into one. My role in the cosmic puzzle became clearer with each passing moment. I felt sad having to leave the young family. I wanted to spend more time with them but knew it wasn't the right time. *I will see them again,* I thought, and with that I focused on the highway.

Once I made it to the highway I posed the never-ending question to myself: left or right? *Right,* I thought. With only two nights left I decided to take it easy and camp at Mesa Verde where Carrie and I were the previous year when we met Harold. It would be fitting that I would end my journey there. The drive up the mountain took no time and before I knew it my tent was once again set up for the night.

My day was spent relaxing and touring the ancient sites. Close to dinner-time the rain began. I knew it might not let up so I got out my propane cook stove to heat my simple dinner while I sat under a tree attempting to stay dry. *No stars tonight,* I thought. The clouds were almost close enough to touch; they swirled very close to the ground.

My dinner was ready in only a few minutes as it only needed to be heated. As I looked to the west I noticed there were some breaks in the cloudy sky. Some of the clouds were black as night, while others were very white. It was a strange mix. I ate dinner in my tent and then had a short nap.

When I woke the rain stopped so I went to wash my dishes. As I did I asked, *Will I see you again?*

A booming voice in my head replied, *We will see you later.*

What were they going to do this time? I wondered. I was feeling excited as well as anxious at the same time.

I went back into my tent and lay down for a short time. I was asleep when all of a sudden I bolted straight up. I was frantic and felt the need to open my tent and get out. I shook my head. *What am I doing?* Then I knew. It was time.

I took a brief walk to the washroom and on my way back asked again, *When, will I see you?*

We will begin as soon as you are seated. What they meant, I wasn't sure. The clouds were still thick and low, hovering just above the campsite. When I got back to my campsite I took the three steps up to my tent, then sat on the top step. The instant I sat down there was a huge white streak of light directly over my head. It had no sound with it, so I knew it wasn't lightning. It was the width of six to eight car lanes and traveled parallel to the earth.

I smiled and said, "Thank you." What further proof did I need to know that I was not crazy and everything that was happening was real? Nothing! I sat there looking out towards the clearing in the clouds and saw a star. It was over. From then on I decided to commit fully to doing what they had asked of me 16 years ago: I would write my story so that I could tell people about them. There would be no more hiding from the truth. I had clarity like never before. Although I hadn't gained any new knowledge on this trip, much had been confirmed to me. Everything was as it should be; my path was clear.

I went to sleep that night with the knowledge that my life would be different from that moment onward. It was time to get to work.

My last day in the Four Corners Area was a lazy one. After breakfast I went to tour a few more of the ancient sites but kept the day, as well as my thoughts, low key. After I had dinner I decided to go up to the main washroom and shower area to check whether or not the gift shop had some water. When I came walking out of the bathroom I ran right into the French girl I had met in Durango a few days before. She told me the guys were parked a few feet away.

What a fitting way to spend my last night, reintegrating back into society before I got home. The three young people from Quebec were having a few drinks and asked me to join them. I graciously accepted and spent the whole evening talking about everything, except Aliens. It was perfect for me. After all that had happened in the past two weeks, I needed the complete reversal of my thoughts. I needed time for my subconscious mind to assimilate my spiritually enlightening trip.

The night went quickly and it was time to say my good-byes. As I walked back to my campsite I felt a sense of contentment within myself. *Today I let go of the old, and am now welcoming the new.* With that in mind I fell asleep with a smile.

COMMUNICATION WITH ORBS

The start of 2005 began with a new focus: to continue writing the book. Writing my story became my priority so I could share my experiences with the world. Subsequently, my life began to change its direction and at times it was difficult to stay focused on the goings-on of daily life.

Seeing the Hopi man, Robert, in 2004 confirmed my feeling that it was time to share my life story. My first step would be to reintegrate into the UFO community. I decided to go online and look into whether or not the annual conference I attended in 1991 was still happening. Once I found that it was, I gave them my address to send me information on upcoming events. This was the perfect first step in becoming involved with like-minded people again.

It was near the end of January when I went to my mailbox and found a brochure from the UFO Congress for an upcoming event. When I pulled it out of my mail slot it was half opened so I examined it more closely. The fact that it was from the Congress and it was open made it somewhat suspicious. Could it be possible that it was starting again, my mail being opened as it came across the border?

I was slightly thrown by this open envelope and, regardless of the reason, saw it as a sign that I should consider going. I made a call to find out more information on the event to see if it felt right to attend. I had a wonderful conversation with one of the coordinators, Adam. We talked about the very first conference I attended in 1991. He had been with the conference from the beginning, which was encouraging as I found the first one very good. It's amazing to talk with people that have no negative judgement and I don't have to feel guarded around. I enjoyed my conversation with Adam, feeling comfortable with him. It was enough for me to decide to register for the conference.

I shared with Adam a few of the events that were happening in my life and we reminisced about the first UFO Congress that took place in Tucson, Arizona. I told him a little about the men that I call the clones.

He was fascinated, but I was sure he had heard many strange stories from people over the years and this one was just another one to add to his list. After our conversation he asked me to make sure I came and introduced myself to him at the conference.

While registering, I asked to be set-up with a roommate to make the conference less expensive. I was a little nervous about the idea but decided if I didn't like the person I was partnered with, I could spend a lot of time out of the room.

A few days before the trip I received a call from the conference. They told me the name of my roommate: Vanessa. She had called ahead to say she wouldn't be arriving until about 1:00 am the first day. She wanted to let me know she would be late so I wouldn't be startled when she came in. It was then I let go of my worry about whom I had as a roommate. It was obvious from her thoughtfulness that she would be great!

Late in 2004 a friend sent me a book in the mail as she felt I should have it. I usually didn't read books but since she sent it I thought I should at least look it over. When it came I could easily see why she thought I should at least have a look at it. The author, Larry, had some wonderful ideas about ETs, but it was a fictional book. Regardless, I felt a connection with the author and, after finding his contact information at the back of the book, decided to write him. I thought he might be interested in helping me write my book. Shortly after I sent the email we spoke on the phone. After a lengthy conversation he said he wasn't interested in helping me write the book but thought maybe we could still meet. He would be attending the conference so we made plans to connect when we arrived in Laughlin. I looked forward to sharing my complete story with him.

I used my birthday as a cover for the trip, as the dates coincided. I didn't want to explain to people at work why I was going to Nevada. Really, I wasn't lying. The trip was a birthday gift to myself as much as anything else. That didn't make it any easier to hide the truth from the people in my life whom I respected.

On March 5th the plane took off from the airport and once again I was on another journey towards finding my place in this world. For some reason I felt it was important for me to be at this conference, and that this reason would reveal itself to me when the time was right.

The flight to Las Vegas was smooth and the plane landed on time. I picked up a rental car and drove two-and-a-half hours to Laughlin. As I drove into the multilevel parking lot at the Flamingo hotel I couldn't help but notice something that made me shake my head. There were a number of cars that had "US GOV" plates on them. *Why are they here?* I thought. I called my good friend Dan and told him about all the government cars; somehow I was not surprised by the their presence.

It didn't take long to find out that the military was currently in the conference room that we were to use. They were having open recruiting for three days. As a result of this, the conference got off to a late start because they still had use of the room. After they were apparently gone I noticed the plates on some of the cars in the parking lot were missing. Many cars were left parked without plates and these cars didn't move for the remainder of the conference.

I gathered my things from the car and went into the hotel to get my room key. As I stood in line for the front desk, I noticed three military-looking guys sitting close to the main desk. They appeared to be keeping a close eye on the line up of UFO attendees checking in.

I looked over the line-up and was impressed by the diverse group chatting excitedly about the UFO gathering. As I listened to some of the conversations I immediately felt happy to be there. It was going to be great! In 1991 I felt comfortable, as though I was among family. I already knew this conference would be the same. After getting my room key, I was off to get settled in.

Over the next couple of hours I unpacked my things, looked over some brochures and had a shower. This wasn't just a holiday it was work as well. I called the front desk to find out if Larry had checked in yet. I took a deep breath as I was connected to his room. As the phone rang, I wondered how our meeting might impact me, or him.

My conversation with Larry was brief and we set-up a time to meet the next day for breakfast. I was relieved that we would be meeting first thing in the morning so I could complete my first task quickly. Now that I was organized I felt I could take some time to walk around and see the hotel and surrounding area. I knew once the conference started I would probably not have time to look around. I would be too busy.

As I walked around the hotel I began to see the name badges of people who were attending the conference, but I stayed to myself. Day quickly turned to night and I went back to my room to take my mind off the reason for my trip. Some TV would do the trick. *This will be an intense week,* I thought.

It was late when my roommate came walking in the door of the hotel room. She explained she had been on a trip to South America before the conference. We introduced ourselves and then had a great conversation before falling asleep. I was happy Vanessa seemed normal—there was a real possibility she may have been one of those over-the-top, way out there types. You never know who will show up to these things; unfortunately, there are some really crazy people that are always in the crowd.

I woke early the next day and went to meet with Larry. Over breakfast I shared with him my story and he was a gracious, patient listener. It was time for the first speaker and I knew he wanted to go but as we reached the scheduled time he said not to be concerned—he wanted to hear the whole story. It had been a long time since I shared my story in such detail. It was a wonderful release and I thanked him for listening. Our conversation was an excellent beginning for my time at the conference; it helped me to remain balanced and calm for the rest of my time there.

After we shared our stories with each other it was time to go to the conference. Before we left, Larry told me there were some people at the hotel that he thought I should meet. He spoke about them briefly and said I should probably just meet them myself. I felt connected to these people, already, from the little Larry told me as he spoke highly of them.

I met with the group, one at a time, throughout the next few days. They had traveled from New York to be at the conference. I connected with a number of them in a way that was comforting and beautiful. Two of the members opened up me in an affectionate way. It seemed they both had received clear messages that they were to travel to this event and that they would meet someone there. Rhonda, the woman, was clearly moved by our meeting. She knew it was me whom she was supposed to meet as soon as we began to talk. She was deeply touched by our initial conversation and I was grateful she was there so we could indeed make contact with each other.

There was a second member of the group, Dean, with whom I had a similar conversation. He told me that he too had received a message that he should be at this event to meet someone. He felt it was me as we began to talk! I told him that I was happy he had come and maybe we were meant to meet. He was an exceptional person who showed an understanding of this world that many people never achieve. He was very spiritual and his demeanour was as gentle as a butterfly.

Both Dean and Rhonda were beautiful people with whom I could see the Aliens had had a positive effect. They were strong in themselves and in their beliefs. It was refreshing to talk with them and know that they were comfortable with the knowledge they held within. So often people feel the need to search through books or anywhere they can to find answers. Dean and Rhonda knew a very important secret: true knowledge comes from within. Books can only *guide* us until we find that place within that releases the information we truly seek. Everything we search for is there.

The more people I met, the more comfortable I became and I remembered why I loved the conference in 1991. It was a short break of the daily ritual of hiding my true self from the world. The people who attend these gatherings freely talk about their experiences and beliefs without fear of ridicule. I was happy to let go of the feeling that I had to guard myself from those who would judge me. It's easier to say someone is crazy than question the possibility that Aliens do exist.

I could see that since I was last involved with any UFO people, there had been a lot of knowledge sharing as well as spiritual growth that had taken place. I was happy to see and hear that the understanding of who the ETs were had expanded. The speakers at the conference were more informed and the people attending represented a wonderful cross-section of society. Doctors, teachers, mothers and working class people: they were from all walks of life. It was obvious to me how hard everyone had worked to educate people on Alien existence. I knew I could have been a part of that group but the time hadn't been right for me to begin speaking about my experiences before now.

Most of the speakers were researchers, with the exception of a few experiencers. Time for speaking had been set aside for contactees/abductees who were at the conference as guests. If they chose to, they could share some of their experiences with the public. Still, it was only a beginning. Raising mass consciousness is a slow process

As the days passed I thought more and more about my friends, the Aliens, whom I call *The Caretakers*. Halfway through the conference I sat in my room, contemplating them. The people who attend these events work hard to teach the general public about Aliens. I sat quietly and cleared my mind. As I went into a meditative state I asked the Aliens to show themselves to this group. The people at the conference had done so much to get the ETs' messages out to the public. The people deserved to know that the Aliens were grateful and supportive. As I opened my eyes I thanked them for showing me that they support me.

I did a similar meditation just before I had left Vancouver to come to the conference. If there was one thing I had learned over the years, it was that nothing is impossible! All I can do is ask and hope to get an answer one day. After I got up from the bed I let the thought go and began to refocus on the rest of the day.

When I went back downstairs the conference was in full swing. There were people mingling in every corner, having conversations with old friends and new acquaintances: clearly one of the reasons people attended this event year after year.

I had seen Adam, the conference coordinator, a number of times since I arrived but he always seemed too busy to talk. I then saw him looking relaxed and in casual conversation so I took advantage of the moment and introduced myself. We had a brief, but friendly, conversation and shared with him an idea that I had been pondering. I thought that a guided meditation with everyone could do a great deal to strengthen the flow of positive energy. He said he thought that was a good idea and asked me to write it out as a proposal so that he could bring it to the conference council. When he asked who I thought should lead this meditation if the council agreed, I told him I thought the guide wasn't as important as the meditation itself.

My brief conversation with Adam came to an end. He had to run off so I thanked him for his time and told him I was glad to have had the opportunity to meet him in person. I went straight back up to my room to write out the meditation proposal. I made it as brief as possible so they could see the simplicity of this important act in bringing people closer together.

That evening there was a dinner for everyone who attended the conference. It was a fun night that gave everyone the opportunity to relax in conversations and enjoy the company of the group. I saw Adam again and presented him with my handwritten idea. I could tell he thought it was good, but it had to be approved by everyone who ran the conference. He told me he would let me know what they thought in a few days. I thanked him for his time and went back to my table.

The rest of the evening was interesting as I took the opportunity to observe the attendees. The diversity of the group never ceased to amaze me. I must admit that I could see there were a few people that were *not all there*. These people are in every sector of society, so it's only reasonable to expect their presence in this group as well. Sadly, it's these people that are often the ones who get the most attention from critics of UFOs and Aliens.

The days of the conference passed quickly and I felt like I never wanted to leave. I thought about the day I would go back to Hopi and wondered how many of these people would be there with me in the future. Many people at this conference have a knowledge that makes many other people afraid. They fear what it is they do not know or understand. This fear is manifested in the ridicule we all have to endure as abductees and contactees. At the conference, for a brief time at least, we, as a group, can be ourselves.

The last day of the conference arrived. I knew that most of the people I had been spending time with wanted to see the speakers that day, but I had no interest, so I headed for the pool. After all, I needed to get some colour on my white skin. I didn't want to miss out on my last chance for a little sun before going home.

When I arrived I didn't notice any conference attendees at poolside. There were a lot of young people splashing around, having fun in the water, so I walked over to the corner of the pool deck where it was a little quieter. The sun was strong and it was very hot.

I got a chair and laid down to soak in the sunshine. My thoughts were on the past week's events and all the people I had met. I thought about what tales I would tell my employers when I got back home about my trip. What could

I share that wouldn't give away what I was really doing on this vacation? My heart felt heavy from just thinking about it, I didn't like having to hide.

The hours of the afternoon trickled away as I got hotter and hotter. To cool off I went for a dip. After the short swim I felt great and I went back to lie on my pool chair. It wasn't too long, however, before I was tossing and turning in the heat. The sun was almost too much to handle and it was extremely bright. Every time I would begin to think of leaving I would have the strong feeling that I should stay for just a short time longer.

It was difficult to open my eyes for any length of time at all because the sun was so strong. Even with my sunglasses on and looking in the opposite direction of the sun, it was still exceptionally hard to keep my eyes open longer than a moment or two. It was strange that it was so blinding.

I turned over onto my back once again, trying very hard to get some sun on my face. It was difficult because of the glare. From out of nowhere, I heard a voice, very loud and clear in my head, *Pay attention to the sky we are coming out!* I knew right away that it was the Aliens! The voice was the same one I always heard when they communicated with me. I sat up on the chair and put my sunglasses on. It was so bright I could barely look up, even with the glasses on. I had to put both my hands up in front of me to try and block the sun so I could see in front of me.

I looked and looked, *Where are you?* I thought. There was no reply.

Then, to the right of my hand I saw something that looked like a ball floating in the sky. It was traveling in a straight line at a consistent speed. Behind it was a second ball. I looked around the pool deck to see if anyone from the conference was there. I wanted to yell out to the people at the pool but I was sure they would then zip off and I would look like a fool. I watched the round orbs drift slowly past, staying in perfect formation to one another. *Why is no one here to see this!* I thought. *What is the point if no one else is here?* Then I wondered if this display was because I asked them to show themselves during this conference. *Thank you,* I said. Then I thought, *No one will believe me!*

I then heard the voice again, this time calmer and quieter, reply *Take a picture.* I had forgotten that my camera was beside me. I quickly took it out and snapped two pictures. By the time I did this, the round orbs were behind the hotel, no longer visible.

I jumped up with my camera in hand, taking a closer look around the pool deck to see if I could see anyone from the conference. Across the pool was a man I had seen attending some of the lectures. I began to walk over to him because I had a feeling the display wasn't over. As I scanned the sky I spotted them on the opposite side of the hotel. I picked up my speed to reach the man before they were out of sight again. *Someone needs to see this with me!* I thought.

"You're with the conference right?!" I didn't wait for a reply. "Get up, quick! You have to see this—get up, get up!" He stood up, somewhat confused, as I pointed frantically at three of the orbs floating by. "LOOK! There!" He jumped up and couldn't believe what he was seeing.

In the sky were three more orbs, shaped differently than the baseball-like orbs of a few minutes before. Rather, these were what I call "star" orbs. They looked exactly like stars, remaining in perfect formation to each other as they drifted past at the same height as the others that had gone past on the other side. I ran out of the gated pool area to see if I could get some more pictures. I only managed to get one before they disappeared behind the hotel. When I returned to the man I found he was very excited and couldn't believe what we were witness to. In between our comments of shock, he introduced himself as George.

The two of us stood at the pool, scanning the sky for any more signs of them, amazed at what we had just witnessed. I was exceptionally excited, recalling how I asked them to show themselves at this conference. Once again my head twisted in all directions. Could they really have come because I asked? Why was that so hard for me to believe? After all I had experienced up to that point, I smiled and thanked them in my mind for coming out.

I was eager to share this experience with people at the conference, so I said good-bye to George and told him I would see him later at the closing dinner. I walked away from the pool with a great deal of satisfaction and excitement and went straight to the conference area to look for all of my new friends. I found a small group of them standing in the lobby area. I walked over to them and began to tell them about what had just happened. One of the people I first told was Adam's wife. She strongly encouraged me to go and tell her husband. I felt like screaming I was so excited, I wanted to share this news with the entire world! The group met the news that the ETs had displayed themselves to us all with excited chatter. What a wonderful gift!

I went into the room where the exhibitors' tables were and found Adam just where his wife said he would be. "Something very exciting has just happened!" When I relayed the story to him I included how, before I left Vancouver and once again in the middle of the conference, I asked the Aliens to show themselves to this group. I could clearly see he was touched by this event as much as I was. He asked if I had a digital camera so he could see the pictures. Sadly I had to tell him that I didn't. I felt awful that I couldn't remember the name of the man by the pool either. When Adam asked me his name, I couldn't tell him because I had forgotten it in all the excitement. I told him I would recognize him though, and when I saw him again I would have him speak to him as well.

From his inside jacket pocket Adam pulled out my proposal for the guided group meditation. He asked me if I would like to do it that night, as well as tell my story of the orbs at the pool. As he said this I realized that this was my reason for being there. Adam told me he would have to get final approval from the Congress council and would confirm with me that night if it would happen or not, but he told me to make sure I came prepared.

After talking with a few other people who were wandering the lobby and exhibitor area I went back up to my room. I needed to get changed from my pool clothing. I was half changed when a strong urge came over me to go to my car and drive. *Now what?* I thought. "Okay," I said out loud. "You want me to go somewhere, I'll go." I quickly left the room and headed straight for my car.

Once in the car, I took a deep breath. Where was I going? What was I doing? *Follow your spirit Miriam,* went through my mind. I pulled out of the parking lot and onto the main road.

Where to now? I asked in my mind.

Turn right.

Lead me to where you want me, I thought. After only a short time I was out on one of the highways and driving out of Laughlin. I didn't want to take a drive out into the middle of no where and said out loud, "Look, I don't want to drive far, can't you just do whatever it is you want to do closer to town?" It was only a few minutes before I found myself pulling off the highway onto a dirt road.

After a few hundred feet I stopped the car. I got out and began to look around. *Now what am I doing here?* I didn't see anything and asked, "What is the point of me being here?"

In my head I heard, *Take a picture.*

Of what? I asked. I couldn't see anything at all. There was a small ridge in the distance so I looked carefully to see if maybe something was hiding along the rim. I saw nothing.

Once again I heard the booming voice in my head, *It will be on the film.*

Okay, Okay! I thought. I got the camera from the car seat and snapped two pictures, unsure of what might end up on the film. I guess I would find out when I got them developed. Perhaps I imagined the whole thing: I knew that my sanity would either be questioned or confirmed after I had the pictures in my hands.

Despite a strong feeling that they wanted me to stay where I was, I left for the hotel. It was late afternoon and I needed to rest before getting dressed for the closing dinner that evening. As I drove back to the hotel my thoughts turned to the possibility that I may have to speak in front of hundreds of conference attendees. I was nervous at the prospect. I had to do a good job—it was important. I knew that these revelations had taken place for me, but also for the people at the conference. My role in this cosmic plan was finally beginning to surface. The time was now for it to slowly unfold.

Back in the room I spoke with Vanessa about the afternoon's events. She asked me if I thought these orbs could be the work of the government. That was a great concern for her. I knew that there were probably orbs operated by the government, but my memory of seeing them as a child made me conclude that they more than likely primarily belonged to the Aliens.

Vanessa and I decided we needed a short nap before dinner. When we woke we quickly dressed for the evening. When we got to the banquet room, there were already plenty of people seated at the big round tables. I found the group of New Yorkers, and asked if we could sit with them. They had plenty of room for both of us and we shared their table. It didn't take long for the room to fill with attendees. Short conversations erupted as people moved about the room. It was our last night together and I could feel the buzz of everyone trying to get in their last words as they exchanged ideas and addresses.

Once we were completely settled into our seats, I scanned the room for Adam. I had to ask him what the others had decided about the meditation, as well as if I could share the incidents of the orbs with the other guests. I spotted him across the room and went over to talk with him. He told me I could speak about that afternoon but said the Congress wanted me to go up with the other man that was at the pool. I still didn't see him but I told Adam I was sure he would show up at some point. I was told I would only have six minutes to tell the story and do the meditation—not a lot of time, but I was grateful for every second given to me. I felt silly that I still couldn't remember his name. I had been focused on the orbs, not the person.

A short time later, Adam made some announcements to the audience and then introduced me. I was nervous but took a breath and knew I would be just fine. All I had to do was tell the story and try not to over-think. After a quick, guided meditation I relayed how I had gone to the pool and saw the orbs, how I heard the Aliens tell me they were coming out and that there was a man who witnessed them as well. Unfortunately, I said, I hadn't seen him yet, but as soon as I did he would come up and share his story with them. Having the limited time made me more nervous than usual, but I thought I did rather well all things considered.

As I stood up on that podium telling my story to the crowd, I couldn't help but feel proud that I heard the Aliens tell me to watch for them. If I hadn't listened and looked up, they wouldn't have been able to show us that they were there for us. The six minutes went by fast and I could feel Adam standing behind me, telling me to wrap it up. I assured the crowd that once the man who was at the pool with me arrived we would be letting them know so he could speak also.

I walked off the stage and back to my table. On my way a lot of people thanked me for telling them about the experience. I was relieved it was done. Once I sat down, dinner was announced and slowly, table by table, we all went to the buffet for our meals.

The evening was well on its way and there was still no sign of the pool man. I was getting nervous and upset because he didn't seem to be there. I had seen him all week–so where had he gone? I was beginning to wonder if people would think I was making it all up. Everyone asked if they could see the pictures. Unfortunately, I couldn't produce those either, as they were undeveloped.

It was a long time after my speech when, finally, I saw the pool man, standing near the entrance to the ballroom. I walked over to him and explained that Adam requested he tell the crowd about that afternoon. He told me he couldn't do it. He said he was so shy that just talking with me was hard for him, let alone a group of people. Upset, I went to inform Adam. I wanted him to know that the man had arrived but that he wouldn't talk to the group. I was embarrassed and felt as though I was letting everyone down.

Adam told me to try and talk him into it, it was important to tell the people at the conference what had happened. Even though I tried to explain this to the man he still refused. I convinced him to at least tell Adam himself so I wouldn't look like I was lying about the whole incident. As George and I walked towards Adam, he then looked at the man and said, "It was you George?!" Apparently George had been to every conference except the first—so they knew each other. It took some really sweet talk but we finally convinced George to speak to the crowd. We walked up to the stage together, shaking, arm in arm.

George told everyone how I came running over to him at the pool, and how he stood up somewhat confused and then saw the orbs floating by. There was a gasp that came from the audience; they clapped and hooted and hollered. It was amazing! We walked off stage together, both of us glad it was all over. After that we were the belles of the ball. I sat at my table with all my new friends and, as people walked past, they would stop to thank me for sharing my experience.

The evening was just about over and it was only a matter of hours before it was time for me to leave. I had to drive back to Vegas that night as my flight was leaving in less than 12 hours. My bags were packed in my room and ready to go. I initially decided to leave at four in the morning to get to Vegas on time for my flight. As the night went on, I realized that trying to sleep for a couple of hours would make me even more tired. I wanted to spend as much time as possible with everyone before I had to leave, so I decided to leave at 2:00 am instead.

After dinner was over, there were small gatherings everywhere in the hotel. People were having parties and I was invited to a couple of them. Vanessa and another girl whom I had connected, Melanie, decided to check out one of the gatherings together. In the dining room I watched as pens came out and people got last minute email addresses of new friends. I was sad that I would have to go home again. *Why couldn't the world be filled with more people like these?* I thought. As we gathered our things and said our good-byes to the New Yorkers, I had to hold back my tears. It felt like leaving old friends after a short visit, it was difficult!

The three of us then left the ballroom and headed to the hotel room party. We found what was, most certainly, an interesting group of people. The conversations in the room turned to topics like ESP and levitation. As I sat and listened I couldn't help but ask myself, *How did I arrive at this place in life?* My life was so different, I was so profoundly aware of things that the average person would have difficulty hearing, let alone accepting: conspiracy theories, government cover-ups, military involvements. There I sat in a room filled with psychics, ex-military officers, scientists, radio hosts, everyday people and me. What a combination!

Vanessa, Melanie and I talked for awhile before going down to the lounge to see if anyone was gathering there. As we went downstairs in the elevator the feeling I had been having all day kicked into full gear. I knew that on my way home I would see *them.* I told Melanie about this feeling and she assured me that I would be just fine. I think she thought that after the conference my imagination was maybe getting the better of me. I knew that I would be alright, but the feeling was strong and I had no doubt I would be seeing them. I wasn't sure, however, if I would only see them or if they would be taking me. It was one of the two; it was only a matter of time before I found out which.

When we got to the lounge we ran into a couple of the New Yorkers. It was close to two in the morning and I knew that I had to get on the road. I looked around at this small group and wondered when I would see them again, if ever.

The closeness with kindred spirits is undeniable. The bonds I made with them would be with me forever in the same way I still have strong emotions about the very first people I ever met that had ET experiences. As much as I wanted to, I couldn't stay, I told them all that it was time for me to leave.

I hugged everyone, tearing up as I walked away. I didn't turn around because I knew I would break down. The front desk brought my car to the door and helped me with my bags. My sadness was a sweet sorrow. I had made new friends and felt at peace for a week. Now it was time to turn my thoughts to the world I was returning to.

Laughlin lights were in my rear-view mirror in no time at all. Usually I loved the feeling of being behind the wheel of a car—but not his time. I didn't like to drive at night and with the feelings I was having about seeing my Alien friends I had no idea what to expect.

Several cars passed me since I wasn't driving fast. I'm not a speed junkie and usually go the speed limit. At night I tend to be even more cautious. After only about 15-20 minutes of being on the road a vehicle came up behind me. I wanted them to pass, so I slowed down. Even at the slow speed they didn't pass. It was jet black out and no one was on the road except the two of us. I wondered if maybe they didn't feel comfortable passing so I waited until a passing lane came up, all the time watching them in my mirror.

They still didn't pass with a clear passing lane. I slowed even more until it was painfully evident that I was being followed. I shook my head and thought to myself, *How stupid do they think I am?* I slowed again. Still, they stayed behind me! I slowed to 20 miles an hour, on the highway, and then pulled the car over to the shoulder of the road. They had to pass now. I gave them no choice unless they wanted to stop with me.

Finally, the vehicle pulled parallel to me and slowly drove ahead. The white van had a license plate that read US GOV. I yelled a few choice words at them as they passed. Then I stopped the car and waited for them to round the corner out of sight before I began to drive again.

The rest of the trip to Vegas was strange. I knew the road looked different in the dark, yet I still felt out of place. It took a lot longer than it should have to get to Las Vegas. Nothing looked familiar. I was beginning to think I might miss my flight when finally I began to see familiar ground and I knew that Vegas wasn't far off.

I didn't see any more suspicious cars. I looked out the window constantly for a craft or some sign of them. I saw nothing. As I got closer to the heart of Vegas, the feeling that I would see the Aliens suddenly grew much stronger. I kept feeling like I should be somewhere—but where?

I finally said aloud, "Look, if you want me to be somewhere, just lead me! I can't look out the window anymore—I will crash this car! I am too tired!" I watched closely for my exit, yet, when I saw it I just kept going for some reason, without any thought at all. After I drove past it I knew that it was probably meant to be. *Now, where am I going?* I still had to take the rental car back and I didn't have a map of the area. This made me nervous. I saw the lights of the Vegas Strip off in the distance. The airport was close to that and so was the car rental. If I headed for the lights I would be okay.

I saw another sign for an exit but, by the time I realized where it led to, it was too late to make the turn-off. In my head I said, *Lead me to where you want me to be. I will listen.* After a couple more exits, I finally pulled off the freeway. The road took me on turn after turn. As I drove I knew I was going in the right direction. I kept driving until I came to a large intersection with a gas station on the corner. When lost, what better place to ask directions?

I pulled in, parked the car and stepped out. I now knew that I was exactly where they wanted me to be. The lighting around the lot was very bright. There were lots of lights outside the building and the gas pump area. When I looked in the direction of the building, I could see a star low in the sky, just above the building. As soon as I laid eyes on it, I knew it was not a star! I looked up to see a second orb directly above me and a third orb to the left. They were all very bright and, considering all of the light pollution and how low they were, they were definitely not stars! "Hello," I said looking towards the orbs.

Okay, I said in my head, *now what?*

Take a picture and just watch, I heard. Well, that was just silly. I couldn't sit in this parking lot at the gas station staring up into the sky and not have anyone notice. Everyone would think I was crazy!

I see you, I know it's you but I'm not going to sit here and watch you! Once again, I wondered if I would be able to share this moment with people or if they would just think I was nuts!

I still needed to know how to get to the car rental business, so I had to ask directions. I had three options: the limo driver filling his car with gas, the taxi driver standing beside his vehicle or the attendant inside the store. I chose the taxi driver who gave me very clear directions. I felt confused because the spot I was at looked somewhat familiar; I was fairly sure I was to go the opposite direction from what this man was telling me. He repeated the directions again, then a third time. "You got it right!? You're sure?! Don't go the other way okay! Do you understand?" He was so adamant that I had to promise him I would follow his directions to the letter!

I hopped back into the car and off I went, ready to follow his crystal clear directions. When I turned off the street I was on, I immediately smiled and said, "Alright, what do you want me to see?"

The taxi driver gave me directions that put me on the other side of a chain link fence that had the Vegas Strip in the background. Slightly above it was the star. I smiling and even chuckled a little bit. *Why not?* I thought. *After everything that happened at the conference with the orbs, why not here again?*

I stopped the car and got out. As I stood at the fence the familiar voice said clearly in my mind, *Take a picture.* I did so without hesitation but questioned why. No one would believe this, no one. How could they? I was alone and a picture of what looked like a star wouldn't be proof of anything. Then I heard the voice again. *Take pictures over time. The progression of light of the sun coming up will show that it has not moved.*

So, there I stood and waited for a short time and then snapped my second picture. The flash went off again and all I could think was, *This won't work! My camera isn't that good!* After about another five minutes I heard a scream in my head, *You have to get out of here, right now, or you will be in big trouble!* I grabbed my camera and jumped into the car as fast as I could. The door was almost closed as I looked up towards the fence. There I saw a police cruiser on the other side driving slowly past me. The driver tried to get a good look at me as I slowly and calmly drove off.

It was then that I took notice of some of the area. There were warning signs on the fence—what they said I didn't have time to read completely. To the left on the other side of the fence were many parked cars. I knew that this was part of the airport and I had been looking over a big open field towards the Strip. Where was I? *Perhaps*, I thought, *this was where people park their cars to take off in those big white planes that they say go daily to Area 51.* I was now fully awake and freaked out!

I had to take more pictures so, for the next hour, I drove in a big circle over and over, stopping every once in awhile to snap pictures. I asked for directions again only to find that my original feeling was correct. If I went the way I originally suggested to the taxi driver I would have been at the car rental place in less than two minutes. Instead I was now looking at this strange star orb that didn't move, hearing a voice speak to me in my head and taking pictures that I wasn't even sure would turn out! Crazy!

The sun was now fully up and yet the star orb had not moved! I couldn't wait any longer. I had to take the car back or I would miss my flight home. I had a strong feeling they wanted me to take more pictures. "I have to go now. I can't wait any longer, if I do I will miss my plane and I don't have the money to buy another flight!" I said out loud. I stopped looking at the orb for a couple of minutes. I drove around the block and, one minute later, the star orb was gone! I had watched it for at least an hour and it didn't move an inch. The minute I decide to leave, it disappears! It was them! Now all I had to do was develop the photos to prove it was the Aliens' orb.

The car rental was only moments away and, after I returned the keys, I had 20 minutes to wait until my shuttle took me to the airport. I stood in the parking lot needing a release, so I called Vanessa, as I knew she would still be in the hotel room. I tried to convey to her the events that took place after I left the hotel but I think I only freaked her out even more with my talk of the orbs. She thought they may all be the work of the government. It didn't matter to me. I was able to speak freely with someone who wouldn't judge me. That was enough for the moment.

The flight back to Vancouver departed on time. While I was in the air all I could think about was the past 24 hours. I had been privileged to see the orbs, not once but twice. If they showed up on my film from my car ride outside Laughlin that would make it three times. I saw the events that led me to this place in my life stacked up in a row like dominoes. When would they all come crashing down? If the orbs were on that film, I would at least have some sort of proof of my sanity! I kept telling myself, *I am the sanest person I know!* As frightening as that may sound, I know it's true!

Once I arrived home I slept for the afternoon. The film with the star was on my mind as I tried to sleep. Who could I get to process the film? Once I awoke I made a call to a friend-of-a-friend and attempted to tell her, in a frantic and irrational manner, the events that had allowed me to get the photos. I made a fool of myself! Once again, I was left feeling out of place and already longed to be back with people that knew and accepted who I was and what I believed. I learned from my interaction with this friend-of-a-friend that it's up to me to feel comfortable, not for others to make me feel comfortable. It was a valuable lesson.

After that I decided to walk up to the pharmacy to get my film developed. I told the man who was processing my film that I wanted all the pictures, even if they came out black. I also told him I wanted them right away no matter the cost—and not to let anyone else pick them up. I knew I sounded paranoid. I tried to keep the negative thoughts away, reminding myself that I was not insane. I left the pharmacy and went back home to wait.

An hour finally passed and I walked slowly down the street, almost not wanting to see what might have turned up on the pictures. This moment was an important one for me. Why they wanted me to take the photos was not clear; but there was one thing I knew for sure: if it wasn't clear now it would be when the time was right.

After paying for the photos, I took a deep breath and picked up the small package from the counter before walking out to the sidewalk. I felt light-headed as I walked down the alley on my way back home. Slowing my pace, I opened the envelope to see the pictures now exposed. I flipped past the many pictures of the people I met at the conference before I saw it.

There, clearly, in my first picture at poolside were the two round orbs. I could also see the three star orbs in the second photo. The two pictures I took blindly as they had requested on the highway outside of Laughlin also had orbs visible in the pictures, just as they said they would be. The truth was there in front of my eyes, an orb on each photo! I stopped in the alley, tears in my eyes. I looked up to the sky, "Thank you! Thank you!" I said in a whisper.

WALKING A NEW PATH

Life after the UFO conference was filled with a lot of excitement. It didn't take long for my new life path to begin to unfold before me. After only ten weeks I put all of my belongings into storage and gave notice to quit my job. Now with no ties to keep me where I was, I had the freedom to listen to the guidance of my soul. My mother's health hadn't been good for some time and I had great concern for her well-being. She was still living in the small town where my Alien contact began, so many years ago. I knew I also needed to go back there to search for the object the Aliens asked me to bury when I was 4-or-five-years old. This wouldn't be an easy task, as I knew it would take me some time to excavate the area in order to find it. With both of these facts in mind the decision to move back to Cranbrook was an easy one.

I knew that once I returned to Cranbrook to be with my mom it would be difficult to leave her to do any traveling. I had been offered an opportunity to meet with a writer in Roswell for the Annual Roswell Festival. I thought it would be a great opportunity to go back to the Southwest one more time to charge my soul with its energy.

With no job, no home and very little money I sat at my friend's computer and looked over the itinerary I had chosen for the trip. It would be three weeks in the most beautiful place in the world for my soul: the Four Corners Area. This was a great beginning of a new life for me.

No longer was I going to hide my truth from people; it was time to get to work and begin to share my experiences. As I stared at the computer, I lifted my right hand and extended my index finger to hit the key to accept the itinerary on the screen in front of me. I took a deep breath and, exhaling, I said out loud, "In two weeks I will have no home, no job and no money. I am now ready to do your work. I hope that you will be there to support me." I pressed enter and in that single moment, I felt my life change. The decision was final; I felt relieved that there was no turning back and no more hiding. I felt a sense of freedom but knew it would be a slow progression towards finishing the book.

I still had about two hours before I had to go to work so I took my friend's dog for a short walk. While we were in the park a voice in my head said, *Look up and you will see us.* As I did in Nevada I listened and began to scan the skies.

I don't see you, I thought.

We will see you later, boomed in my head. I kept searching the skies all the way back to my friend's home but saw nothing. I then had a short rest before work.

At about 4:15 pm I left the house to walk to the bus stop where I was taking the bus to work. It was a perfect day; the sky was crystal blue with a few white fluffy clouds nearby. As usual, I kept my eyes to the skies. Really, I didn't expect to see anything. I turned onto 49th Street and walked to the bus stop. As I stood there waiting, I looked up. It was then I noticed two bald eagles circling just above and to the left of me.

My first thought was that this was a good omen. The last time I had seen two eagles was just before my first trip to Arizona, back in May 2003. I smiled and thanked the eagles for being there for me to see. I did a quick glance down the street for the bus and, when I looked back up, the eagles were gone.

49th is a busy street in the middle of the city. Vancouver is known as a green city with lots of trees. The houses that lined this street had large hemlock tree growth all around them. Thinking the huge cedar hedge beside me hid the eagles; I walked 30 feet to the street corner to get a broader look at the sky.

As I looked straight up I saw above me a star orb and one round orb, silvery green in colour. *No way!* I thought. They hovered on the underside of two big white puffy clouds. They didn't move but stayed in a fixed position. *Is that you?* I asked. It was 5:00 pm, the sky was crystal blue and the sun was out—there would be no stars at this hour! I was sure it was them! *Thank you, thank you,* I said in my mind, smiling ear to ear.

I took a couple of steps closer to the street corner while watching the orbs as I reached in my pocket for my cell phone. I tried three friends only to find no one home. I wanted to share this moment with someone. Finally, I reached my friend Shannon. Just as she answered the two orbs began to move toward the Earth. They both began to move at the same moment and stayed in perfect formation as they descended.

I relayed to Shannon everything that was playing out in front of my eyes. At the exact same time both the orbs stopped moving just above the tree line. They were now across the street from me, near the back end of a home, about four storeys high in the sky.

I was very touched by this event and asked the orbs, *Do you have a message?*

The response was as clear as the voice in Vegas, *We are always with you.* I began to cry, not because I was sad but from pure gratitude and happiness. How fortunate I was to have this happen to me! When I sat at the computer only two hours earlier, I asked them to support me. They certainly showed me that I am never alone. They are always with me no matter where I am or what I am doing. It was an indescribable feeling of love that came over me.

I was still on the phone with Shannon, telling her how close they were to me. The orbs were now both stationary. After a moment the round orb began to move. I wasn't sure what it was going to do as it picked up speed and moved closer to the star orb while traveling parallel to the Earth. I thought for a split-second that the two would merge. Instead, it went under the star orb and kept going until it was out of sight behind the tree line.

The star orb didn't move for another couple of seconds. Shannon couldn't understand why I was crying. I tried to tell her it was because I felt so fortunate! I don't think she understood my response. I looked down at the ground and wiped my eyes of their tears and when I looked back up the star orb was gone.

It was time to get off the phone and get back to the bus stop. *How did I arrive at this point in my life?* I wondered. I felt blessed and knew that the path in front of me was the right one. There would be no more waiting; nothing could have been clearer than the fact that I had chosen the right path to follow.

I went to my job that night and was very quiet. I watched all the people and tried to imagine what they would do if they had my life. Would they go crazy? I had seen people lose touch with reality over experiences far less strange than mine. I must be somehow important to the Aliens. They kept making that clear to me. That afternoon they had given me another sign to stay focused and keep following my spirit.

The two weeks of work went quickly and, before I could relax, I was off on another airplane to the Four Corners Area. On this trip, as with all other trips, I had only an idea of where I wanted to travel. I have learned over the years that if you plan every moment you will miss everything that may be waiting for you. Although I had a list of places I wanted to see, my spirit would have the final say as to where I went and what I did along the way.

I landed in Albuquerque on June 30th where I went directly to meet with Harvey, a writer I met at the UFO Congress in March. We connected at the conference and I initially thought he might be interested in helping me write my book. When I found out we would both be in New Mexico we made arrangements to meet again in person.

He would be waiting for me at the car rental area. When I got there he was sitting on one of the big couches lining the window area. He quickly jumped up to meet me and before I knew it, we were off on the highway on our way to Roswell.

Harvey was filled with questions for me right from the beginning. I found it difficult to explain my views to him about certain aspects of my beliefs as well as my experiences.

He was extremely analytical, making me unsure of whether our partnership would work. Our thinking was opposite enough to make for great writing but the process could be too difficult.

I spent the next few days in Roswell wondering what on Earth I was doing there. Harvey listened to many of the speakers while I was left to roam around on my own, as I was not interested in most of the lectures. Since 1988 I have had knowledge that has only become somewhat accepted in the last few years. From the beginning I made a promise to myself not to over-indulge in other people's information. Many see this as being foolish; they wonder why I wouldn't want to learn anything new. It is very simple: I have all the information I need. My experiences have been extensive and detailed, why would I want to have someone lecture me about the reality of my own experience? Why would I want someone to tell me that my experiences are good or evil? I know what I have experienced. No one on Earth can take that truth away from me; I will be my own judge.

Even though the festival was going on until July 5th I didn't feel right about staying until the end. I woke in the morning of the 4th and had the overwhelming urge to leave. Harvey had rented the car from Albuquerque so I had no way of getting out of town. This, however, didn't present a problem as much as it did a challenge. I knew that with the strength of my feeling to leave, a ride would present itself to me.

As usual I was correct: a wonderful artist I met offered to drive me to Albuquerque. When I told Harvey he became upset. The purpose of being at the festival was to meet with Harvey and see if maybe we could work together. Although I found him to be an exceptional writer, I had the strong impression that I needed to write the book about my experiences on my own. My hope was that Harvey would be understanding of my insight.

The drive to Albuquerque was a long one but I enjoyed my time with the artist. He was a very kind and interesting man. When we finally arrived it was dinnertime and, after I rented a car for the second leg of my journey, we both drove to have dinner together. We had a wonderful conversation and dinner was excellent. I knew that this would be my last meal for some time that wouldn't be camp food.

After dinner I had to get on the road if I wanted to get anywhere before I got too tired. The sun was low on the horizon as we stepped out of the restaurant and walked back to our cars. I was happy now that I felt free of any restrictions. I decided to start driving towards Chinle and see where the road led me. We said our good-byes and I jumped into the car, ready for another adventure.

As the sun went down I got very tired but I kept driving. I had the feeling that I had to get to Canyon de Chelly before I could rest. It was comforting to know where the campground was and that arriving late would not be a problem. As I pushed myself to the limit I finally arrived at my favourite campground at one in the morning. Exhausted, I pulled into the campsite and fell asleep in the car.

I woke to the sounds of flute music. It didn't take long for Stevenson to come over and say hello. He told me that I had arrived on the right day: there was going to be a Sweat Lodge later that afternoon. Stevenson chuckled as he told me that the person who originally requested the sweat lodge had asked for it to be postponed a day. Furthermore, the Medicine Man had also said to Stevenson that it would have to be changed to a day later than it was originally scheduled. Stevenson said that they must have been waiting for me. I smiled as I thought of everything I had been through the day before in order to get there. If I had left Roswell on the following day as originally planned I would have missed it.

I spent the day relaxing and catching up on my sleep from the night before. Before I knew it, Stevenson was beginning to prepare the fire for the Sweat Lodge rocks. I walked over and asked if I could help. He was pleased and so I began to drag wood over to the fire pit. As I did, a woman came over and began to help as well. She introduced herself as Chantelle. She told me how she had been traveling and camping all around the Four Corners Area. I could clearly see that she was on her own spiritual journey, searching for some food for her soul, as I was.

After the fire was going well, Chantelle and I went back to our tents to change in preparation for the sweat. When I arrived back at the lodge I was amazed to see that a man from Europe, whom I had met last year, was there. We began to talk and he said to me that I must have a strong spirit because nothing had gone right for them to have had the sweat the day before.

The Medicine Man arrived and talked with all of the participants for a few minutes. As he prepared some herbs for the sweat I asked him what they were. I told him that if he didn't want to tell me, I would respect his decision. Not only did he tell me, but also he gave me a piece of it and told me to taste it. I was very touched by his openness and thanked him. After he walked away, Stevenson said I must be very special, the Medicine Man won't even tell him when he asks. That meant a great deal to me—but, in some strange way, I was not surprised.

The sweat lodge was exactly what I needed to begin my journey into the Four Corners Area. It was an amazing release for me and helped me to focus. The Ceremony ended and we all went back to our campsites to get cleaned up before rejoining each other for the traditional mutton dinner.

As with the year before, I found that the people at the dinner had a special open bond with each other. It was a wonderful experience despite my fatigue. While everyone was beginning to leave for the night Stevenson came over to me and asked if I would participate in a ceremony that he had asked the Medicine Man to do. I felt honoured that he asked since this would be a genuine Navajo Ceremony. I said yes with the knowledge that I would never be able to tell anyone any details about the ceremony out of respect.

I had to make a quick trip to my tent before the ceremony began and I walked with Chantelle. We stood and talked for a few minutes. She made some very interesting comments to me, considering she knew nothing about me. She said that she was amazed at how Stevenson and the Medicine Man interacted with me. She was envious of the clear connection I had with the Navajo people.

In the darkness she said, "It's almost as though they recognize you or something—like you being here was preordained." In that moment I knew that she had a good connection with her spirit, even if she didn't recognise it. I told her I wanted to tell her a story before she left the next morning. We said good night and after a quick trip to my tent, I went to the Hogan, a traditional Navajo home, for the Ceremony.

After the Ceremony with Stevenson and the Medicine Man I had a deep and restful sleep. When I woke, Chantelle and I had coffee together. She wanted to get on the road so we exchanged email addresses with one another. She was taken aback by the brief outline of my story and then told me that she could tell there was something different about me. When she left the campground, I enjoyed the rest of my day around the Chinle area with Stevenson.

The following day I called the Anderson family to let them know I would like to come out to see them in Colorado. They had bought land near Durango, close to where we met the year previous. They had planned on camping there for the summer and invited me to camp with them. It was perfect timing since it gave them a day to get settled on their new land before I arrived. I was excited to see them again.

Early in the morning I left Chinle and arrived in Colorado around noon. After traveling in circles for awhile I finally found the Andersons' land. As I turned the corner off the dirt road onto the private drive, my heart began to speed up. After I had met this family the previous year, I began to write my book, sending them my story as I wrote it. When we met I had said nothing about Aliens, so I was sure they would have a lot of questions. I was as happy as I was nervous and excited.

I drove very slowly since the road was rough. When I turned the last corner I saw them all standing beside their travel van. With them was a girl whom I did not recognize. They all looked up and waved as I pulled up beside them.

Jason and Kathleen seemed as excited as I was. Jason introduced his niece, Leanne, to me. She looked to be in her early twenties and, as I had with their daughter, I felt that she was another amazing extension of this family. I knew instantly that this would be an interesting visit.

Over the next couple of days I shared the stories of my life with the Andersons. They, in turn, shared with me their philosophies on life and what had led them to this land in Colorado. Sustainable living was their original reason for buying the land. Their ultimate goal was to eventually leave the bustle of the city where they currently lived and begin a more peaceful and fulfilling life. Jason, Kathleen and Leanne were students of the Earth, constantly learning how they could leave the fewest footprints on it as possible. Homemade soaps, natural building, and medicinal herbs—these were only a few of the topics they shared with me. It was very clear as to why I was so drawn to these people when we had met at the campground outside Durango. If I could envision the type of person that the Aliens wanted their message to go out to, it was people like the Andersons.

Leanne was an interesting young woman and I felt a real connection with her. She had the spirit of a warrior: strong, determined, and focused. The other side of her was like that of an angel: delicate, passionate, and filled with compassion and love. She talked constantly about her love of the planet and how she could almost feel its pain over how society had begun to destroy her. It was obvious to me that she was one of the light beings on the Earth, here to help bring the people back to a peaceful existence on the planet. When I meet young people like Leanne it gives me hope for the future of humanity. Her strength and knowledge of the way we should be living gives everyone around her strength.

Living in harmony with the Earth; remembering and learning the old ways; giving thanks for everything this wondrous place supplies for us—today we call it sustainable living. With all that I had been told by the Aliens, I could see that this family was following their guidance, even if they did not know they were—settling in the one place I was told were the Safe Lands: the Four Corners Area.

As my time with the Andersons came to an end I couldn't help but smile inside. I was so happy that I made the decision to meet with them in Colorado. I felt very close with Kathleen; she was like a long lost sister to me, as well as a mother at the same time. I never told her this, but I felt safe being around her.

Everyone knew that I was going to go and see the Hopi Medicine Man again—the question was when. After two wondrous days in Colorado I woke in the morning and knew it was time to go. Kathleen made breakfast for everyone and we talked about my next stop, Hopi Land.

I was nervous about going to see Robert again. This trip was like an unscheduled visit as there was no need for me to go there, at least not from the Aliens' perspective. The visit was solely to pacify my human emotions. Although I didn't need any more confirmation, I wanted it.

The drive to Hopi was beautiful; I passed the red rock mesas and, as always, took a deep breath as they came into view. I loved the feeling of being in that area: it felt like I was coming home. It's a comfort that is not easily described.

From Colorado to Hopi I had to pass Chinle, but this time I would not be stopping to see Stevenson—that would have to wait until I was on my way back through. The closer I got to my destination, the more my mind turned to what I would say to Robert once I arrived. I knew that the book was already being written about my experiences and that I would have to release it to the public within the next year. My intention was to tell Robert my goal and see what kind of a reaction he had.

The red sun began to say good night to the Earth. As I drove, I saw Robert in a vision: he was going to be leaving his home soon. I didn't want to miss him so I drove a little faster, knowing that he would be leaving in 30 minutes. My eyes kept a close watch on the time but, as the minutes passed, I knew that I wouldn't catch him. I hadn't told him I was coming, believing that if my spirit wanted me to talk to him he would be there when I arrived.

As the car pulled onto the mesa I knew I had missed him by about 20 minutes. My hope was that he would at least be coming back and hadn't gone on a journey of some kind. I pulled the car in front of Robert's home. As with the last time, all eyes were on me as I got out of the car.

Darkness had set in and as I approached Robert's door I could see that it was also dark inside. I went to the door anyway, just in case. It was open so I peeked my head slightly inside to call out a hello. There was no reply.

The year prior I was taken to a relative's home across the street for breakfast. I knew they would probably know where Robert was. The home was filled with the bustle of children. Before I could knock on the open door, several of the people inside were already greeting me at the doorway.

"Hello," I said.

They looked at me and said, "Hello."

"Do you know if Robert is around or is he out of town? I think I missed him by about 20 minutes."

The woman had a confused look on her face. "Did you have an appointment with him?" she asked.

"No, I just missed him didn't I?" They looked at me strangely.

"He went to the Kiva."

"Okay, I can come back. Do you know how long he will be there?"

Before I knew it, they were sending one of the kids to the Kiva to tell Robert I was there. I don't think they even asked my name. All they knew was a strange woman was there to see him. I told them I had been in their home for breakfast with Robert last year. Some people spoke in Hopi and then I heard Robert's voice behind me.

"Hello! Hello! Come on." Robert waved his hand for me to follow him back to his home. As we walked in the door he giggled and said, "What are you doing here? I didn't expect you until next year!" As he said this, I chuckled inside. I knew this was an unscheduled stop.

I sat down with Robert who was smiling from ear to ear. "What are you doing here? What's going on?" he asked me again.

I told him, "I am here because I started to write about my experiences. I wanted to tell you and the Hopi people. I am not here to ask your permission. I don't need to ask your permission because what I am writing about is my life. I am doing what the Aliens asked me to do and I follow them."

"Okay, but what can I do for you?" Robert asked rather seriously.

"I don't really know—I guess I want to know if the Hopi are going to accept what I write about. I'm here to tell them I am doing this."

It was then he gave me what I came for. "Do you want me to gather the Elders? I could do it right now if you want? I don't know what you want. Maybe you want to talk to them one-on-one to see what each one of them knows, or maybe you want to speak to them as a group. You let me know," Robert said while leaning towards me.

It was clear to me that Robert felt as I did: maybe, just maybe I was someone important to the Hopi people. The secondary reason I came to Hopi was so I could feel the land again. When I went to my hometown to look for the gift given to me by the Aliens I wanted to be able to think of the land here as I thought perhaps it could help guide me to the gift. I wasn't sure if any of this really made sense at the time, but it felt right, and that was all that mattered. I was following my spirit. Knowing how to follow your spirit—is a key to this life.

"I don't need to see them now, it's still too early," I told Robert. I wasn't sure why I said these words. Sometimes I will say things when I am in a certain frame of mind that I feel don't really come from me. Instead, the words come from my spirit. I really wanted to talk to the Elders but somehow I knew if I did the Aliens might not be happy with me.

"How long are you going to be here? Are you going to take off again?" Robert asked. The year before he really wanted me to stay for the celebration after the ceremonies but I knew I couldn't. I told him I would have loved to stay but the time wasn't right to meet everyone. This time, I said, I would be staying for as long as it took. I had lots of time and I was in no rush. He offered me his home; gratefully, I accepted his hospitality.

I felt I had been given a gift with Robert's presence, as he was busy doing ceremonies in the Kiva with other Hopi later that night. He told me I could stay in his home as he went back to the Kiva. When he returned we talked for a few hours about what had transpired for both of us since we had last seen each other. I shared with him that when I returned to my hometown I would begin to look for the object the Aliens gave me as a child.

Over the next couple of days Robert and I talked mostly about the Aliens, but not entirely. I felt like I was home again. Each morning we would go to his relative's home for breakfast. I was sure everyone was wondering what I was doing there, especially because he was letting me stay in his home. The second night on the mesa Robert asked me if I would like to go for dinner at the restaurant a short distance down the highway. As always I didn't have a lot of money and was trying to eat only camp food to keep my costs down, so I was grateful for this outing.

As we were about to get into my car on our way to the restaurant, the Hopi woman from next door began hollering at Robert in Hopi. I could tell they were talking about me because they kept looking in my direction and then back to each other. Robert laughed as he got in the car. As we pulled away I asked him what she said. "She told me to get rid of you. She said you are no good. You can't even cook me supper—you have to take me for supper. She said it was time for you to leave the mesa," he said with a smile on his face.

"What did you say to her?" I asked, returning the smile.

"I told her that you aren't taking me to supper. I am taking you," he replied. "Oh they are all talking, everybody, before I even got down into the Kiva last night the questions started," he said, chuckling again.

"What do you tell them I am doing here?" I asked.

"I told them you are here just to talk—boy does that get them!" Robert replied.

"They keep asking me as well what my business is with you."

"What do you tell them?" he asked.

"Well, I tell them the same thing, that I am here just to talk with you." We both laughed. We were keeping everything a secret and it must be driving them all crazy, we concluded. *In time,* I thought, *I will be able to speak freely.* I wanted it to be that day, but I knew it wasn't the right time. For me, for the Hopi, for the Aliens—who knows, but I had to wait.

After two nights on the mesa I knew it was time to get back on the road. I wanted very much to stay but there was no real point to it. I got what I came for and it was time to move on. Robert and I spent our last few minutes together talking about my eventual return. I told him the next time I came back I would be staying. More importantly, I would be sharing my information about the Aliens with anyone who wanted to hear it. He seemed pleased with that and we sat in silence for the last few moments before saying good-bye.

Once again I found myself looking at Robert through my rear-view mirror as I drove off the mesa. This trip to Hopi had been calmer than the last visit. I felt my mind and body starting to come together with my soul and I could feel the harmony beginning. No more hiding, no more waiting—the time was close at hand now.

I quickly turned my thoughts to the next leg of my journey. I still had several days before I was to return home and I was grateful for the opportunity to relax. I felt as though the rest of my time in the Four Corners Area could be spent taking it easy. I decided to make one last stop in Canyon de Chelly and see Stevenson before moving on to Colorado to spend my last days with the Andersons, camping on their land.

The drive from the canyon to Colorado was restful and, as always, beautiful. By now my path had taken me on the same roads so many times, I could no longer count how often I had passed the red rock mesas. The bold rust colour was magnificent against the blue sky. Each time I saw them it was as if it was the first time.

I didn't feel as though I was on any kind of timeline, so I drove slowly, taking in the sights. At one point near the Arizona/New Mexico border, I pulled the car over to have a rest. I was in the middle of nowhere—a great place to be. Unable to see any buildings of any kind, I wanted to take in the solitude of my location. It was stark desert land with foliage scattered about in the mid-afternoon sunshine. I got out of the car and stood at its side.

I pondered the last few days' events with Robert and wondered if I would indeed ever be living in this wondrous universe of desert. Even with the stark scenery I could still feel the energy of the Earth. It's like a song being whispered in your ear, calling for you to sing in harmony with it. I am sure that anyone who is at all spiritual that travels this area feels the Earth calling them to stay in the desert. Until people experience it for themselves there really is no way to convey its full effect on the soul.

It was almost time to get back on the road when I did a double take of something to the right of the car in the near distance. A star orb floated past. "Hello," I said to it and smiled. I shook my head and wondered how I was so fortunate to see them again. In a matter of a few seconds they were gone and I was off to see the Andersons.

I arrived back in Colorado in time to join the Anderson family for dinner. I felt blessed that they were being so kind to me. Throughout this trip many people gave me free camping and food. I was extremely grateful for all of it! That night over dinner I told them how my visit with the Hopi Elder went.

Leanne, Kathleen and Jason were happy I came back to share with them my adventure to Hopi. I explained to them it wasn't as exciting as it was on my last visit. I was calmer and more focused. I went on to tell them how the Hopi man offered to gather the other Elders for me to talk to but I had declined. There really wasn't a lot to share with them at that time.

Before we all went to sleep late that night, we made plans to drive to Mesa Verde the next day. I was looking forward to seeing the ancient Anasazi sites again. I began to think about Harold and how we met there two years prior. As I drifted off to sleep I could feel that moment again, remembering how it helped shape my life as it gave me confirmation of the information the Aliens told me in 1988.

I opened my eyes to the sunshine and heat of the morning. It seemed like I hadn't even slept. A simple blink of my eyes and I was waking to a new day. The Andersons were all moving outside the tent, already making breakfast. When I stepped outside I was welcomed with warm smiles and the smell of brewing coffee.

After coffee and a quick breakfast, everyone jumped into my rental car and off we went to Mesa Verde. The drive to the highway turn-off wasn't far from our campsite. Along the way we saw a bald eagle circling in the distance further down the highway. We all decided that this was a good omen. I was unsurprised by the sighting. I reflected on seeing the bald eagles in Vancouver just before I saw the star orb in the middle of the day at the bus stop.

The excitement of seeing the bald eagle kept the conversation going until we arrived at the turn-off to Mesa Verde. As we drove the winding road up the mountain I took in the surprising changes that had occurred since my last visit. The brush seemed to have grown higher and was greener than the previous year. The dead, statuesque trees from the fire were somewhat less noticeable.

As we took the last turn before reaching the tourist center I looked to my left, out the side window. I did a double take. There, not far from the car, about 100 feet away, going in the opposite direction, were two star orbs. I shook my head in disbelief, thinking that maybe it was a glint off something that I was seeing. I tried to keep my eyes on the winding road while trying to get a better look at the orbs.

On the third look I told Jason, who was sitting in the front passenger seat, asking him to look out the window to the left. I tried to point out the orb to him. Unfortunately I was too late, they were too far away in the distance and no longer visible. I felt sad that Jason was unable to see the orbs since I felt they may have shown themselves for his benefit.

After another couple of minutes we were at the tourist office. Jason and I stood outside, waiting in line for tickets for a tour. Shiprock was far off in the distance, draped in a gentle haze of purple, making it look mystical. I took in the view while thinking about the star orb. Suddenly, in the distance in the same direction I saw another orb going past again! I couldn't believe my eyes! I blinked and lost it for a moment before catching another glimpse of it.

I knew that if I wanted to show Jason or anyone else I had to act quickly. I grabbed Jason by the arm to turn him towards the orb. It was so far off in the distance that it was hard to keep track of, blending itself against the stark desert ground and the bright sunshine of the late morning. "Look," I said to Jason as I pointed with my finger. "There is another orb, can you see it? It's almost gone!" He eagerly searched the skies with his eyes. I stood closer to Jason, trying to have him follow my arm to my fingertip in pointing to the orb, but sadly he was unable to see it. I wasn't surprised since it was barely visible even to me.

Leanne, Savannah and Kathleen came to stand outside with us. Shaking my head, I told them how I had just seen another star orb and that I tried to point it out to Jason. I couldn't help but think that he was meant to have the opportunity to see them.

I was happy that the Andersons were enjoying their time on the mountain with the spirits of the past. It was an honour to be able to walk on the soil, see the sky and touch the earth at the ancient sites where there was a strong feeling of mystical power.

The day passed quickly and it was time to head back to camp. Once we arrived everyone busied themselves cooking or setting up for the night.

Upon my return to Vancouver I knew I had a couple of weeks to tidy up loose ends and prepare for my move to Cranbrook where I would be looking after my aging mother. My sister was kind enough to agree to pay for the plane ticket to return home. I had left a message for Janice to wait until she heard from me before making a final purchase for the plane ticket to Cranbrook. As I waited for dinner to be ready, I borrowed Jason's phone to call Janice. I thought it would be a short call but, after she told me she already bought the ticket, I became upset and told her that I would call her back. Knowing the conversation would take longer than a couple of minutes, I wanted to drive to the nearest pay phone so I could charge the call to my home instead of having the Andersons pay for it.

Twenty minutes later I was standing at a gas station telephone talking with Janice again. We argued for a few minutes about the plane ticket. Finally, I realized that it was already booked and paid for and so there was nothing more to talk about. I couldn't change what was done and I needed to be grateful that she paid for the ticket in the first place.

I was still very upset as I drove back to the Andersons' campsite. Suddenly, I noticed the words of the song on the radio station. "Why are you so sad? You are safe with Kathleen. Close your eyes and put your head in her lap. She will comfort you. Do not be sad—you know you can see what is on the horizon. The ships are there in the distance and are on their way to you now. We know you miss your home; we miss you too. You can see upon the horizon the ships will be there to take you home. Do not be sad. Look to the west and the ships will be there to take you home. Watch for them—they are grey."

It was just a woman's voice; there was no music in the background. *Strange for a rock station!* I thought. *What just happened?* When the song ended, a hard rock song came on the radio. I don't like to jump to conclusions, but I couldn't help but wonder if the song was some sort of message. It was not the normal way messages came to me, through the radio or the television. This was a first for me. As I went over the song in my mind, I couldn't find any other reasonable explanation for what I just heard, other than it was the Aliens. *This was very weird!*

Once I arrived back at the campsite I quickly told the Andersons about the song I just heard. They all thought it was very odd as well and were surprised I remembered as much of the wording as I did. *How could I not?* Clearly, it did not belong in the normal context of the radio station's music and so I paid special attention. Not only was it void of music, the words to the song were not at all normal as well. The only reason I paid attention was because it was completely out of place. It was like finding a block of butter in your bedroom dresser drawer.

I was very happy to spend my last night in the Four Corners Area with such amazing people. Our last dinner together was a time of reflection over the past three weeks. This journey had been a transition point for me. I knew that upon my return I would begin working on the book. Where this path would lead me would reveal itself in time.

The next morning I packed up my things and put them in the car for the last time. It was hard to accept that I had to leave and go back to Albuquerque to catch my flight home. After all, I felt like I was already home. It was a hard morning and an emotional one for me. I lingered as long as possible before I knew I had to say good-bye. As I gave Kathleen, Jason, Savannah and Leanne a hug, good-bye tears overcame me and I had to jump in the car and leave quickly in order to avoid a scene.

As I drove away I looked in the mirror for the last time to see everyone waving good-bye. *I will be back,* I kept telling myself, *another day, another year.*

The drive to Albuquerque was uneventful and the flight home even more so. When the plane touched down in Vancouver I felt focused on the immediate future. Work was on my mind almost immediately. I wanted to make some money before going to Cranbrook and I only had a couple of weeks to tidy up all my loose ends. After all, I had no idea how long I would be in Cranbrook once I arrived.

THE SEARCH BEGINS

It felt like I had just landed in Vancouver and there I was, already on a plane to Cranbrook. Janice was at the airport to greet me and bring me to my mother's home, it was August 1st, 2005, one month short of the twenty-year anniversary of leaving Cranbrook. It was a strange feeling to be in my hometown again, this time to stay.

The drive from the airport gave me an opportunity to see the beautiful mountains that surrounded the area. I had always loved looking at them as a child. On every visit I took to Cranbrook they would capture my attention as much as they did when I was young. I used to daydream, wondering which animals lived on the mountain, imagining beautiful meadows filled with wild flowers at the top.

As we pulled into the driveway I could see my mother in the window. She was already smiling in anticipation of seeing me again. As I walked through the door to the house I could feel my life's direction shifting. This was a new beginning and partly reinforced my commitment to the requests of the Aliens.

My mother was very happy that I was back in her home to stay. The room lit up as I walked up the stairs and gave her a big hug and kiss. She was beaming with happiness over my arrival and that made the first step of my move to Cranbrook a good one.

My goals were clear. My priority was to help look after my mother and, just as important, I was to look for the object the Aliens had left with me as a child. I had to work on writing the book about my experiences. My last goals were to take some classes at the community college and look for a job.

I shared these goals with Janice and, to my surprise, she had some thoughts as to where I had buried the object. She told me in her own words where she remembered me hiding it. The exact details she gave were the same as I remembered. After showing the gift to Janice, I placed it in an old white cloth before placing it in the ground. I told her she wasn't allowed to touch it and we both had to make sure that our father never found out about it. I then put it in the hole I dug in the Earth and covered it with rocks and soil.

Even though I remembered my sister being with me as I buried the object I didn't think she had any memories of the event. What she had remembered included the detail of the white cloth as well as having to hide it from our father. I was amazed! When I asked her exactly where it was she confirmed its location for me—her memory was exactly the same as mine.

Never before had Janice and I talked in detail about this object. Having her input was important to me and motivated me further. There was a slight problem, however. Janice had a vague memory of moving the object. As soon as she told me this piece of information my heart sank: how was I going to find it if she had moved it? My first thought was for hypnosis to recover the memory, but I could never ask her to do such a thing. It would be like asking a person to open Pandora's box—once it's open she could never close it.

There was no point in digging for the object until I had more information from Janice. So I waited, patiently. I knew an answer to the problem would surface in time. A week later, Janice came to tell me she thought having hypnosis may help her remember where she moved it. I was very happy that she came to the decision on her own with no influence from me. Now all I had to do was find a hypnotist that I could trust with such delicate information. I knew that this task in such a small town would prove to be a challenge.

Over the next week I focused on finding the right person to hypnotize Janice. At least twice a day I meditated on the universe to bring the right person into my life. Near the end of the week my efforts were rewarded. Through a strange set of circumstances I found myself talking to a woman with whom I had had a brief encounter in Vancouver 15 years prior. It was through our conversation that she brought up the name of a counsellor, Helen, who also did hypnosis. I knew she was the right person to help Janice as soon as she told me about her. The circumstances in which she was being introduced to me were rather amazing. I knew my request for a hypnotist had been answered. Now all I had to do was meet with her to confirm she was indeed the right person for the job.

That afternoon I went straight home and made an appointment to meet with Helen the following day. I was excited since this would bring me one step closer to finding the object I buried as a child—one step closer to my possible fate.

From the moment I laid eyes on Helen I felt comfortable with her. However, I needed to talk with her to confirm my intuition was correct. We sat in her living room and had a long conversation regarding the reason for the need of a hypnotist. I told her about the Aliens and my family's involvement with them. She was very open and accepting of the whole story. Helen then quickly and excitedly agreed to try and help Janice remember details of where the object was.

She asked Janice and I to be as specific as possible about the date on which the encounter occurred. If we had the exact date, it would help Helen to be more specific and she wouldn't have to use any leading questions during the hypnosis. I was very adamant that she not lead Janice in her questioning in any way. She needed to be very careful with what she asked.

Janice and I couldn't come up with the exact date but we both knew that I was either four- or five-years old. That meant it had been 1970 or 1971. We wondered how we would ever figure it out. If I was patient and held my faith, the information would come to me somehow.

We had to wait a couple of weeks, anyway, in order to set up a date to begin the hypnosis sessions. In the meantime I focused my thoughts on trying to pin down the exact date of the abduction as a child. Janice and I talked about the time of year and determined it was either early fall or spring. There were no vegetables in the farmer's field so we knew the time of year was as accurate as it could be. How to determine the year was another matter and we both said we would focus on trying to remember more details.

It was only a few days after I spoke to Helen that I went to visit Catherine and James Johnson, Gillian's parents. Gillian was my childhood friend and, at the age of 12, I had lived with them for about a year. Life at my parents' house was difficult. I was extremely grateful when they took me into their home with open arms. They really were like a second family to me.

Since my return to Cranbrook I had visited Catherine and James on a couple of occasions. It was a nice surprise to know they still had a place in their hearts for me. One of the things I wanted to accomplish in moving back to my hometown was to tell some of the people from my past about my Alien experiences. I knew it would be difficult and that I was setting myself up for ridicule, but I needed to take the step.

On my way to the Johnson home I decided that I would tell them about my interactions with the Aliens. I wanted to be honest with them and was as prepared as I would ever be for their reaction.

After an hour of us all playing catch-up I felt it was time to begin to tell them my story. I began by asking them to allow me to tell them the whole story before asking me questions, otherwise I may never get to the end.

Shortly after I began, they interrupted and told me they believed me! It helped me to relax as I wanted to tell them everything I could in the short amount of time I had. After two hours of me recounting highlights of my Alien interactions, Catherine took me by surprise.

When I was very young the Johnson family lived down the street from our family. The community we lived in was very small and I have memories of many of the families in the area. Catherine began to tell me she remembered one of the area residents telling anyone who would listen about seeing a UFO hovering over the field in front of our home. Apparently, he talked about the UFO sighting for years. No one ever listened to him because he was an alcoholic. Everyone thought he was seeing things. When Catherine told me this I asked her if she remembered what year it was. After some thought she told me, to the best of her knowledge, the year was 1970.

I had the sensation of tingling all over my body after I listened to Catherine's story about the UFO. For years I wasn't clear on whether I was four- or five-years old. Now, there I was, finally having another person confirm my age. I was very happy about this new piece of information and shared my excitement with Catherine and James. I told them this was the information I had been looking for in order to pinpoint the date of the Alien encounter as a child. It was amazing how much of that particular night was clear to Janice and myself. Our memories were identical and now there I was, 36 years later, finding more corroborating evidence of the events of that fateful night. I knew now that I was four-years old at the time of the encounter. This knowledge meant that Helen could better guide Janice in recovering her memory.

Catherine and James shared their views and beliefs about UFOs and Aliens with me after listening to the end of my story. I was overwhelmed by their openness and acceptance of me because they were important to me. I had a great deal of respect and gratitude for everything they had done for me as a child. If they had thought I was crazy, it would have made me very sad. Now I felt as though I could be myself and share my life with them without hiding anything.

After hours of talking about the Aliens, I had to be on my way. As I left the Johnson home I hugged both Catherine and James, telling them how much it meant to me that they accepted me and, more importantly, that they had accepted my Alien story. I left with feelings of excitement and relief: excited that I had one more piece of the puzzle in finding the buried object, relief at their acceptance.

The following day I called Janice and told her about my conversation with the Johnsons. We talked about that night as children out in the farmer's field. We both remember feeling as though the world around us was sleeping, as though not even the creatures were moving that night. So why did this man remember seeing the UFO? The only logical conclusion was that maybe he was so drunk at the time that the Aliens couldn't put him to sleep. Janice was pleased at knowing the year in which my abduction took place. Now we could call Helen and set up the appointment for the hypnosis sessions.

When I called Helen she told me it would have to wait at least two weeks. After 36 years of waiting, what was a few more months? There was no rush for us since it would be months before we could begin digging. The earth needed to soften enough to begin working with it as it was early fall. That meant we would have to wait until spring to begin the search. In the meantime, all we could do was wait.

A week later Janice called me in the late afternoon. A friend of ours, Kelly, who had lost a loved one the year prior, was asking if the two of us could go with her to spread his ashes in a special place. I had received messages from her partner in the previous year and passed them on to her. For this reason she asked me to participate in the Ceremony.

An hour later Janice arrived to pick me up with Kelly and her sister Yolanda. The four of us began our drive out of town on the highway. The night darkness was creeping in and as it did I began to gaze out the window of the truck. As usual I was looking for the stars to come out and say hello to the world. I thought, *This would be the perfect opportunity for them to show themselves to Janice since we are going out to the middle of nowhere and no one will be around.* I kept that thought for the next hour as we drove, leaving civilization behind, heading into the backcountry. *It would be a good idea for Janice to see you again. We are going to do a Ceremony and you must not interrupt it but it would be good if you showed yourselves tonight.* I kept this as my mantra for the rest of the drive.

After an hour and a half we finally arrived at our destination. The truck stopped beside a riverbank and we all stepped out. I looked upward and around. I could see a ridge of mountains and hills that surrounded the area and it was very dark. The stars were now out in full force and it was really beautiful to see them twinkle in the night sky.

Kelly left the truck rather quickly and walked to the river's edge. She was crying heavily and we all let her go off on her own. I said to Janice, "Don't be surprised if you see them tonight. I just wanted to let you know they may show themselves and if they do don't freak out."

We were at the site for less than 5 minutes when Yolanda began to holler, "Oh my God, look! It's a UFO!" She turned to us and pointed to the orb moving across the sky. Janice and I just looked at each other, smiled and shrugged our shoulders.

In my mind I said thank you to them and then said aloud, "Will you stop for us for a minute? Or will you at least slow down for us?" As I said that they slowed but kept moving. Yolanda couldn't believe what she saw. The star orb looked like a ball of light low in the sky, passing over us with no sound at all. Yolanda kept asking if we saw it, wondering why we weren't jumping up and down with her over the sighting. She was taken aback because the orb appeared to listen to my request to slow down.

Both Janice and I told Yolanda we did see it and that it didn't freak us out. We were very casual about it. At that moment we heard Kelly crying and we all dropped the UFO talk and decided it was time to go to her. As we did I said thank you to them again for showing themselves. I was happy the Aliens sent a probe to us and I kept an eye on the sky in case they came again. I repeated in my mind that they were not to interrupt this Ceremony because it was sacred. They couldn't overshadow the purpose of us being there.

The three of us stood at the riverbank as Kelly stood in the water talking through her tears about her loved one. She then released his ashes into the river; by this time we were all in tears. As Kelly walked back to shore we walked towards her and all began holding hands, standing in a circle.

As the four of us stood in the darkness we bowed our heads and each of us said a few words of good-bye. I opened my eyes and looked up. As I did, I could see two balls of light coming towards us. It was two more orbs. I quickly said clearly and sternly in my head, *You must go back, you must not interrupt this Ceremony. It is sacred to us and it is not right for you to come at this moment!* The one orb farthest away blinked to black and the one closest to us stopped and then began to travel back to where it came from. I thanked them once again in my mind for leaving and my focus went back to the group.

When we all finished speaking, we made our way back to the truck. It was very cold and was getting late. I had to go to the washroom before we headed back so I went to the back of the truck to do my business. As I did I tried to keep my eyes on the skies. Very quietly I asked them to do a fly by with the craft. No one was around and I wanted to see them. *Who knows when the next time I may be in such a remote area.* As I stood up I looked directly above me. "Wahoo!" I yelled. From one mountain ridge on the left of me to the other mountain ridge on the right was a huge streak of orange light. It was so fast and wide it was amazing! It had to be at least 100 feet across. There was no way it was a meteor. It was too low, too big and went from ridge to ridge with no sound: not the normal path of a meteor. I felt blessed and again I thanked them for showing themselves to me.

I walked to the front of the truck where Janice, Kelly and Yolanda were talking. I asked them if they saw the streak of light but none of them had. I wasn't surprised since it happened in the blink of an eye and was silent, but I was also sad they hadn't seen anything. In another moment we were all back in the truck and heading back to town.

The next day I told Janice that the appointment with Helen was coming up and asked her if she was still okay with having the hypnosis. She told me she was up to the task and, if anything, seeing the UFO made her even more comfortable with the whole idea.

It seemed as though the days flew by and before I knew it the day arrived for Janice to have her hypnosis session. When we went to see Helen she asked to talk with Janice alone. When they came out of the room Helen said that she and Janice felt it was best that I waited in another room. After the hour session was over, Janice came out and told me she didn't really get anywhere. No memories came up that were of any help. Not having any answers after one day was not a surprise.

It took another two sessions before Janice and Helen exited the hypnosis room with solid results. Helen in particular was excited by the memories she was able to uncover. I was led into the room and sat in preparation for the great revelation.

Janice and Helen said the object was indeed moved. Janice remembered removing it from the spot I buried it to show a friend of hers. It was then taken by Janice's childhood friend. After recovering the object, Janice then reburied it within feet of where I had originally put it. The only thing she did differently was bury it deeper than it had been previously. This was great news; the three of us were elated. Now all I had to do was wait until spring to begin the search.

I was excited to know where it was and couldn't wait until I could begin digging. I asked Janice to come with me to the site so we could get a feel for the area. When we pulled up to the spot my heart sank as I gazed at the land in front of me. It was completely different from when we were children and it was immediately obvious that this task would be much harder than I had anticipated. Janice and I walked around the area and tried to remember the exact spot we had left the object. The Earth was not as it had been when we were children. A building that once stood on the property was no longer there and a bulldozer had pushed the soil around. *No matter,* I kept telling myself, *I will find it.* After all, why would everything in my life have happened the way it had if I wasn't meant to find the Alien gift?

Janice and I agreed that above all else, we had buried *something* and I was resolved to finding it. All I needed was determination and, oh yeah, maybe a miracle!

At the end of 2005 I was waiting for the New Year to bring spring and begin to soften the earth. In the meantime I focused on the book so I would be prepared for anything that could happen if, and when, I found the Alien object.

(2006)

As 2006 came into view I felt time inch closer to the day I could break ground and search the earth for the Alien gift. Everything seemed to be coming into place and it was only a matter of time before I found what I was looking for.

On several occasions I went searching for the object. On a few of those days Janice came with me as the two of us searched together. Unfortunately, the year passed with no results—but that wouldn't deter me.

Many obstacles came in my path in 2006, preventing me from spending much time at the site. I saw it as a sign that maybe it was too early.

Once again, I needed to sit back and wait—wait for the right time to begin the work again. In the meantime I would focus on the book and keep my heart open for the Aliens to guide me if that was what was needed.

With everything that told me my memories were true: from Janice, my father, the Hopi, Catherine, Harold, and many others, I knew I could never turn my back on any of this. It is impossible for me to do any such thing. So no matter how long it takes I will continue my work in service for the Aliens whom I have come to know as The Caretakers. I will also continue my search for the object and the complete truth to everything I have experienced.

PUZZLE PIECES
INTENTIONS

I wrote this book because of a direct request from the Aliens in 1988 to do so. They asked me to educate people as to who they are and what their message to the world is. Due to many factors, it has taken a long time for me to begin this task for them. Whenever I thought about beginning the book it never felt right, until now.

The reason I chose to write this book in the style that I have—laying out the events that took place rather than rushing straight to their message—is simple. In order for you, the reader, to begin to listen to their messages, you need to first accept that UFOs and Aliens do indeed exist. The reality of the Aliens must first become, at the very least, a possibility in your mind in order for the messages to have any impact on you, the reader.

I have attempted to show you some of the experiences I had in my life in relation to the Aliens. My intention was to show you some of the moments that shaped my perceptions. I have shared a glimpse into my world; everything I have shared with you is factual and the complete truth. I have attempted to demonstrate how these sometimes small events changed my life. How and why I have come to the conclusions I have is laid out in my story.

When you begin to research on your own, and I hope you do, don't let the ridiculous overtake you. If something doesn't feel right, then don't believe it. Listen to your instinct and allow that to guide you in your search for more information. Keep as close to the mainstream in the beginning as possible, as this is where you will find more consistency and accuracy.

Don't think you need to believe everything you read. There are people that use the UFO and Alien concept for attention and/or security in their lives. Ufology is like society: it contains all walks of life—from the rational and believable to the mentally unstable. The more ridiculous the story is, the less believable it becomes. Look for simple answers when beginning your own search for answers.

There has been a great deal of conversation throughout the UFO community over the many different *types* of Aliens that people claim contact this planet. It can become very confusing and even annoying when attempting to learn information about the different Alien races to those in search of more information. Don't allow this confusion to distract you from finding the truth. Somewhere in all the hype, misinformation, and the ridiculous you will find real and honest answers, you will find evidence to support the claims of sightings and abductions all around the world from before the birth of Jesus Christ.

The beings I have had encounters with are about 7- to 8-feet tall, and have blond hair and blue eyes. They are sometimes referred to as The Blonds or Tall Blonds. These beings are the focus of this book and it is their messages I carry. They go by many different names in the UFO community but by putting any further labels on them I find they then take on the blanket of information that has already been written about them. Since some of the information that has been presented to me over the years about one type or another of Aliens I have not always agreed with, I prefer not to label them any further.

The messages they gave me in the past and still give me to this day are of peace, love and balance. I truly believe with all my being that these Aliens have our best interest at heart. They have never asked me to do anything that would harm another person in any way. They have instructed me to teach others about them, respect the earth and all that lies upon it. They have instructed me to obey the laws of the land and its people. Their message is not about disregarding the world; rather, it is about respect and living in harmony with it.

Everything I have shared with you comes from my own experiences and direct knowledge of them. I never have and never will pass on information learned from other sources as being my own.

Why did I write this book now as opposed to any other time? The world is on the verge of a great change and it is time to prepare. We no longer have the luxury of time on our side. We have effected the Earth in such a negative way that she has begun to shake us off her. The prophetic messages the Aliens asked me, as well as many others, to share with the world are now relevant. The signs that the end is near have begun to be seen and recognized: climate change, world unrest, complete disregard for fellow man and disconnect from the Earth itself.

Until recently the warnings and words of the Aliens would not have been listened to at all. The work of many people who have come before me, educating the world about the Alien presence, has laid the groundwork upon which I and people like myself can build. If I had tried to tell this story before now it would have been pointless. We are moving into a very important time on the planet. Our actions in the immediate future will dictate our fates as to whether or not we will survive and go on as a species.

What happened in the hours after the highway encounter in 1988 started me on a journey to find truth, peace, acceptance and understanding. Some of the time I spent with the Aliens that day was clear in my mind from that moment forward. Other parts would take weeks, months and even years to become clear. The events that transpired, as well as what I was shown and told inside the craft that fateful day, changed my life forever.

I can never again look at the world with the same ignorant eyes. Once you know the truth, it can never be taken away or erased. It swims in your soul and nothing or no one can change it. Pandora's box opened and it can never be closed.

When the Aliens shared information with me they gave me the gift of experiencing it as well. In other words, when I was shown a picture of being on board a craft hovering above thousands of people with their arms reaching upward, screaming for help after a disaster hit the earth, *I was there*. The actual experience of that event was given to me.

It is for this reason that these experiences and interactions with the Aliens are so real and affect people so deeply. Imagine living another life and having all those experiences *placed* within you. As an example: you can read books about rock climbing, watch documentaries on it, listen to your friends as they tell you about their experiences climbing—but until you actually do it yourself, you haven't experienced it. Well, this is what the Aliens do. Not only do they give you the gift of knowledge of rock climbing, but the gift of the *experience* of it as well. I am not sure how this is accomplished but I do know it is the reason the information we are told makes it next to impossible to ignore their warnings. We change our lives because we cannot turn our backs on what we know to be the truth.

People who have had these extraordinary interactions with Aliens will almost always completely change their lives after the event as they are compelled to follow the instructions given to them; live good lives, take care of the earth and live in harmony with all things. We are told to respect all that we have: our food, water and this world. We are told our bodies as well as our spirits are sacred and to be mindful that our lives should not be taken for granted.

A question that I have been asked on many occasions is: why do you believe you were chosen to receive these messages? There are many reasons I may have been chosen and all of them are only speculation on my part.

It is my understanding that the Aliens helped to create us. I am not in any way implying that I think the Aliens are God, but I do believe, and was told by them, that they had a hand in creating humankind. This takes me to what people often refer to as a possible genetic program being done by the Aliens. It could be that there are certain families throughout the planet that the Aliens have always monitored since the beginning of humankind in an attempt to modify, and possibly introduce, new genetic strands of DNA into the world.

As I have made clear in my writing, my father has had contact for most of his life with these same Alien beings. It is understandable to assume that this is a strong reason for my initial contact. The reason I have received so many messages and seen them so many times over my lifetime could possibly be because something within my very soul is strong enough to process the information and still remain rational. With each contact I was able to process the data given to me with an exceptional amount of clarity, and so they decided to keep giving me more. This seems to be true with most people in contact with the Tall Blonds. The more information you are able to process and can accept, the more they will share with you.

Was I chosen or did I volunteer? Why was I chosen? Any answer to these questions is only speculation and really have no bearing on the fact that remains: we are not alone.

Can anyone have these experiences? I would imagine that if the situation was right and the timing was right, anyone could be chosen to see the Aliens in their physical form. They can be reached through meditation as well; often this is how they will keep in contact with those who have been taken by them in the physical form. Those people who have contact with the Aliens through meditation can only receive messages as clear as their mind. Messages sometimes do not get through our personal filters clearly and so it is important to always remain objective, even with yourself.

In early 1990 I decided not to read other people's interpretations on this subject so that my mind would remain clear on what took place on the craft that day in 1988. I found it difficult to imagine listening to a researcher explain to me why I had these experiences and even more difficult to imagine listening to another person's interpretations of my experiences. After all, the experiences were mine—a gift to me. If I can't remember part of my experience, why would I accept another person telling me what happened to fill in the gaps? That is not at all logical.

Ufology was an obscure subject in 1988 for the general public, I feel comfortable with all the knowledge the Aliens gave me as being the truth and my memories as clear and correct because of this. Over the years I have read very few books and listened to even fewer speakers talk about the subject in any detail. I try to limit my exposure to them so my memories remain as clear and uninfluenced as possible.

Even when I went to the UFO conferences in 1991 and 2005, I rarely listened to the speakers. My focus was, and always is, on the people who attended these types of functions. I find the people are the reason for the gatherings to take place. It is in the personal interactions with people we find others who are like-minded and/or have had contact from the same group of Aliens.

It is remarkable how the messages given to so many people around the world are often identical. The information that is remembered by a person who has had contact can contain the same phrase regarding a particular piece of information. For example, the phrase, **"NOW IS THE TIME"** seems to be synonymous with many initial contacts. Others, who have had contact with the Tall Blonds, receive messages that are geared towards preparations in the event of a sudden global change. The details of this information are also often identical. The messages the Aliens bring that affect people to the core of their beings are some the most important aspects to this phenomenon. For example: many people are told specifically that in the End Times the Four Corners Area will be one of The Safe Lands.

OTHERS

Since my experience in 1988 I have had the ability, at times, to be able to recognize others who have had genuine experiences, not just at obvious events like the UFO conferences, but in my daily life as well. I have recognized complete strangers as fellow experiencers a number of times at bars, coffee shops and bookstores. I could share several examples of this but have chosen the following two to share with you. I don't always tell the person of my recognition, but on every occasion I have, it has proven to be correct.

One day in Vancouver I went into a bookstore to see what kind of books were being written about Aliens. I never read them, but seeking out these types of books gives me an idea of what kind of information is now being released to the general public. It lets me know what pieces of the puzzle they have been fitting together lately. Normally I only read the cover to get an idea of what the book is about.

There was a man who appeared to be a street person looking at the books when I arrived. He didn't see me but I smiled: I knew he had had contact with Aliens. He put the book down and stepped back. I then picked up the same book he had just had in his hand. As he moved away he said, "It's all real you know."

"Yes I know," I replied as I looked at him and smiled.

He smiled back. As he walked away he said, "Good! Another one of us!" We recognized each other and knew that we were both awake to the knowledge that we are not alone. We recognized the Alien contact in each other and acknowledged it.

Another incident that demonstrates this recognition we have with each other took place in another bookstore. Two blocks from the store I heard a voice in my head, *There is someone you will meet in the store that will be important to you.*

When I entered the bookstore I went to look over the new books that came in and kept my eyes open. I didn't know who I might be looking for but I kept my heart and mind open to possibility. After about half an hour of browsing the book aisles I decided to check out the music section. The moment I rounded the corner I looked up and there she was! *She has had a lot of contact,* I thought, *and I need to talk to her. I would be surprised if she was not fully awake to her experiences. I must not leave until I talk with her!* Not only did I recognise the woman across the room to have had contact, but I also knew it was with the Tall Blonds.

Now the real question was how I would start a conversation with her. After the initial moment of recognition I realized she was an employee. As I walked towards her she looked at me, smiled and said hello. Her nametag said Alma. Before I had time to think, we were engaged in conversation about a piece of spiral jewellery for sale. We discovered it was the spiral symbol we were both attracted to. It was a great way to begin a conversation with Alma and I quickly found her to be a very friendly and interesting woman.

I knew I needed to ask her to meet with me for a coffee so we could talk further—but how would I do that? I didn't want her to think I was strange. Our conversation touched on the Hopi people but neither of us mentioned Aliens or UFOs. We both had deep connections to the Four Corners Area and this helped convince me she had had Alien contact.

I walked to the cash register and she went with me to put my purchases through. She was bold enough to say she thought maybe we should get together sometime and talk. It seemed that we had many of the same interests. It was like a strong invisible string I could feel between the two of us, pulling us together. I told her I thought that was a great idea and I was really interested in talking with her as well. Alma and I exchanged phone numbers and I strongly encouraged her to call at her convenience.

A couple of weeks after I met Alma she called. I knew that we were meant to meet that day. Nothing could have been clearer as we talked about our lives—we quickly found there were many parallels. After talking for some time we concluded that we should meet in person and ended the conversation by setting up our next meeting.

The next time Alma and I met we talked for a couple of hours. It was a very interesting conversation and not at all a surprise. I told her about my Alien contact and she in turn shared hers with me. During our conversation she confessed that as soon as she laid eyes on me she knew I had had contact as well. She told me she had felt a strong push to talk with me and to not let me leave until she did so. There it was: confirmation of everything we both initially suspected. We were in contact with the same group of Aliens and our initial recognition of that was what brought us together.

Alma is a very good friend and confidante to me to this day. She may be a newer addition to my friends, but she is invaluable to me. Her knowledge of the Aliens and her own spirit is extensive. She is a beautiful soul and I am grateful to have her in my life.

WHO ARE THE PEOPLE WHO HAVE ALIEN CONTACT?

It is important to understand that people who have had Alien contact have more to share then just a story about physical contact with an Alien race. What the Aliens *gave* us in the way of knowledge *is* the message. *We* the abductees are *part* of the message and it's time to stop and listen! Every person I am aware of that has had direct *physical* Alien contact changed their lives completely after the event. How have our lives changed? What are our beliefs before and after the encounter? How do we feel about seeing the Aliens? These are only a few questions that you should be asking people like me because the next person it happens to could be you. If the Aliens do have to make themselves known on a global scale to humankind, it would be to your benefit that you, at the very least, have a general idea as to who they are and what they represent.

It is impossible to explain the intimate details of all the knowledge the Aliens shared with me or share completely the abduction/contact experience with these beings and expect you to understand fully. You can't. As ambassadors of these Aliens, people like me had a great deal of information placed *within* our beings. We, as humans, lack the ability to translate that knowledge through words in a way that would be understood. These are their gifts to us as participants in this grand design.

This gift of knowledge is the reason abductees are unable to turn our backs on the requests made by them. *We understand* why they are making the request. The drive we have to complete our specific tasks is almost impossible to say no to. It is made a part of who we are.

Let me share an analogy of the complexity of the information shared with me by the Aliens. The moment you are born you begin the process of being exposed to language. At first it is spoken to you and, as you get older, letters, words, books and numbers all become a part of your world. At first you don't understand any of it, yet somehow you know it is important. This process takes years until one day, all the little puzzle pieces that have been in front of your eyes since birth come together and you can talk, read and write. There is always more to learn of course—languages, styles of writing, etcetera. All the information you ever needed was right there in front of you. You just needed time to learn the *keys* to putting it all together.

So it is with physical Alien contact. We are given the keys to an inner knowledge and an understanding that is far beyond anything words could ever explain. It would take *lifetimes* to learn all the languages of the world. It is as though the Aliens gave people like myself all the languages of the world in one visit. So when we are asked about what we are told it is often unexplainable. All we can do is attempt to explain the information in an *overview.*

We contactees/abductees do not, however, have all the answers. We have each been given specific tasks to help humanity further themselves spiritually and emotionally. We have all been given a basic education of Universal insights and understanding. From there we have each been taught whatever subject area we need to complete our tasks. One may know about technology, where another person knows nothing of technology but rather about star charts or healing. For this reason you should never allow yourself to be blindly led by any one person's ideology about life, religion *or* Alien contact. We are all educated differently and therefore do not have all the answers. We are still human beings and are susceptible to our own misinterpretation as well. I constantly question myself on every aspect of this phenomenon and I ask that you do the same with me or anyone else you research.

I, and people like me, have a certain level of understanding that helps me process an awareness of things that humanity cannot always see. We learn that *everything we do as a collective affects other dimensions and worlds* and this responsibility should not be taken lightly. This is one of the Alien messages.

Most of the people who have had direct, physical Alien contact will choose not to speak publicly. They have to be concerned about being ridiculed by the general public. We may be your co-workers, your neighbour—maybe even your best friend. You may have known us for years and never suspected anything out of the ordinary. We must maintain our secrecy to protect our ability to co-exist in this world.

If, and when, the time comes for the Aliens to make their presence known to humankind on a global scale, we are the people who will step out of the shadows to become intermediaries between humans and the Aliens. Don't be afraid of us. Give us the opportunity to speak. It is what we are all waiting for.

Even though we are the ambassadors of the Alien message, we are not perfect. We are still living in a human body in the physical world and have free will. We are here to learn our own lessons just like everyone else. We simply have a different view on life and it is one that we are waiting to share with the world; when it is time and when the people of the Earth are ready to listen, we, the abductees and contactees, will stand together without fear of ridicule and share our knowledge with you, freely and openly.

MY FATHER

It was in the early days of my contact that I knew just from looking at certain aspects of the phenomenon, that my father must have had contact himself. The patterns I saw in myself, as well as in the people who came to the group abductee meetings in 1990, often made me think of my father. The day after I was taken on the highway I suspected his involvement.

There were many reasons that I felt my contact was carried on through my father and onto me. My father always talked about the end of the world as though it was an obsession. He appeared somewhat paranoid, often claiming that people were watching him. He talked about survival skills and demonstrated ESP ability on many occasions. Often he spoke of having superior genes when compared to other people, and our family lineage apparently had these "special" genes as well. He told us as children that we were "bred" not just born. It was a frightening thing to hear him discuss as a child.

These indicators of my father's involvement may seem insignificant but they are a glimpse of my reasoning after my abduction on the highway. After I began talking with people in the UFO abductee group, I quickly realized I might be right, as others knew that their contact ran in their family history. It was clear during these meetings that we all suspected, or knew as fact, that contact ran in our family lineage. There were also a number of us who recalled contact starting at approximately age five or six and then every six years thereafter.

Another reason I thought he may have had contact was because some of the people I met who said they had contact were crazy. They didn't integrate the Aliens' information very well and, as a result, didn't fit back into society easily after their experiences. Instead the information they received seemed to make them completely paranoid, causing them to become completely unhinged. They could no longer see the line between reality and imagination, allowing the latter to take over. Despite my strange encounters, I first try to find a logical explanation for everything. Then, and only then, do I suspect or confirm Alien involvement.

During my time with the Aliens in 1988 they told me that I was partly of them. They told me they had a part in creating me specifically. From my father's ranting and his reaction to me telling him about my highway experience, I believe that there is a strong possibility that I am a hybrid of the Tall Blond Aliens. After all, my father said he saw them often around the time of my birth. It was then he said they were around him constantly and would not leave him alone. This could have been the Aliens visiting him, or, it could have been because of me.

As for who my biological parents are; there is no doubt that I am the daughter of both my parents as I have genetic, physical traits specific to both. It is for this reason, I believe the Aliens may have altered my DNA in some way after initial conception.

My most recent conversations with my father regarding the Alien contact have proven to be *almost* fruitless. He refuses to give me any more information than he already has. The small comments he has made imply he knows much more than he is willing to share.

Once, as I sat speaking with him he paused and almost held his breath. He let go of a small smile almost like a slight wicked sneer, looked me right in the eyes and said, "The government is afraid of you. They think you are one of them."

"What do you mean?" I asked him, knowing full well what he meant but I wanted him to say it!

"They think you're an Alien, not human, you even look like them, that's why they are afraid of you. You need to be careful. You shouldn't get involved. It will ruin your life and I don't want that for you. This is the only advice I can give you."

For today I must be content with what he has shared with me and hope that in the future he will be willing to tell me more if he knows anything of value or interest about the Aliens or about me.

TELLING MY MOTHER AND SISTERS ABOUT MY CONTACT

Each of my family members reacted in a way that I did not expect when I initially told them about my encounter on the highway. I feel that sharing their reactions may help show how this phenomenon has touched each of them, as well as how it has affected me.

(1989)

It took some time for me to find the courage to tell my sisters about my Alien contact on the highway. I had to assimilate the experience for myself first and then I needed to plan how I would begin that conversation. Since I didn't have the money to fly or drive to Cranbrook to see them in person, I knew my only option was talk with my sisters over the telephone. During my conversations with Janice and Carol I asked that they not inform either one of my parents. I wanted to explain the experience to my mom and dad myself.

After lengthy conversation over the phone, in separate calls, both Janice and Carol's responses shocked me. They both began to cry and said the same thing to me: "You're not my sister! You're an Alien! What have you done with my sister?" It took a great deal to calm them down and convince them that I was, in fact, their sister. This was a very strange response to have, but not completely without reason.

The day after the highway encounter I had changed so much so that everyone around me was concerned. Growing up I had no concept of spirit guides, astral travel, other dimensions or other things of a religious or spiritual nature. I grew up with psychic ability but didn't fully understand it. The day after my abduction my psychic ability peaked and my knowledge and understanding of all things spiritual was suddenly extensive. So extensive in fact that it was as though I was given access to the other side. I was tapped into that clarity for approximately a two-year period after my encounter in 1988. It seemed that overnight I had lifetimes of study of all things relating to spiritual life placed within me. It was extremely difficult to live in normal society with that amount of clarity but it eventually calmed down, allowing me to better assimilate all the information I had been given. That access remains to a certain degree to this day but it has subsided since my initial contact. Some people even thought I looked different after my contact on the highway.

Both of my sisters asked me if I remembered them ever being taken by Aliens. I told them that I have no clear memories of that ever happening. When I was four Janice was with me when I left the house to go with the Aliens in the farmer's field, but they sent her back to our home—she did not come with us. Janice is more intuitive than the average person and Carol also has exceptional intuitive ability. Carol also has some memories that may indicate she could have been taken at some point. She has a clear memory of looking out a window of some type of craft as she is being lifted higher and higher above the Earth. This memory has remained in her conscious memory her whole life. She maintains that it felt like a real experience and it leaves her with a fearful, foreboding feeling.

I assume that if Alien contact has partly to do with an Alien genetic program then it would be understandable for both Carol and Janice to have had some sort of contact themselves. There is little to back up this claim, however, yet it should not be completely ruled out.

TELLING MY MOM

I didn't want to tell my mother about my experiences in a phone call, I felt that I should share my experiences in person with her. I thought maybe, just maybe, she could shed some light on the subject. For this reason I decided to take a trip to Cranbrook. After all, maybe she had been taken as well. If I am partly Alien, as they told me I am, then my mother must have been implanted at some point. Perhaps she had some obscure or strange memory of the event.

As I traveled home, I tried to plan the moment I would tell her. I was very nervous about sharing my tale as I was worried how my mom would react. After a couple of days of visiting I finally found the right moment to talk with her about my experiences. It was early evening and I sat on the carpeted floor in front of her as she sat in her large armchair. As usual I asked her to allow me to finish my story before asking questions, it helped make it easier to explain.

When I was done speaking, her initial reaction was rather calm considering the subject matter. I always considered my mother to be a student of philosophy. As she was well educated in that subject and science. Most of her questions tried to ascertain what the Aliens told me. As I shared with her some of the philosophies the Aliens shared she was shocked. My outlook and understanding of life had completely changed. At one point during our philosophical conversation she asked me if I meditated, of course my answer was yes. She then asked me to demonstrate how I went about doing this. I didn't understand why she was so interested in how I meditated, but I was happy to share with her anything she asked to help her accept and understand what I was telling her.

As I sat on the floor I curled my feet inward in a standard meditative position. I placed my hands on my knees and closed my eyes. I visualized inhaling white light, exhaling white light. I sat in this position for no more than two minutes and, as my mother watched, I could feel myself changing. My body began to tingle all over and it felt as though a cover over my body fell down, exposing my true self.

It was in that moment my mother screamed. "Who are you? What have you done with my daughter?! You're not my daughter—you're an Alien!" I jumped up and followed her as she walked down the hall towards the bathroom, crying.

She was clearly afraid of me and yelled for me to get away from her. When I finally got her to calm down I asked her why she was afraid. "You're not my daughter, I saw you change in front of my eyes! You didn't even look like my daughter!"

It took half an hour to convince her that I was still her daughter and not an Alien. The truth was, the Aliens had told me I was partly from them so maybe I was an Alien after all. I certainly wasn't about to tell my family that information! I eventually asked her what I looked like as I was meditating. Her description was nothing new to me as there had been several people in the past that had watched me meditate and seen the same image of a woman appear in front of them. I appeared as a tall woman with flowing blond hair and bright blue eyes wearing a long white robe.

Telling my family about these experiences was very difficult for me. When I eventually did tell them I was somewhat surprised at their reactions. Even though they seemed to be upset, not one of them told me I was crazy. They all believed me at the time. Their belief in my story comes and goes even to this day. I believe it is fear. After all, if all I say is true, then they have to accept that the world is not at all as it appears to be. To this day they support me and encourage me to follow my spirit to find the truth to my experiences and my involvement in this phenomenon.

I must admit that my mother has no recollection whatsoever of ever seeing anything strange. She does, however, watch every UFO show on TV and listens to UFO radio programs. The only clue I found that may be relevant is a fear she has of flying through the air. Somehow the thought of this seems to terrify her. Again, this is only pure speculation that this is somehow connected.

JANICE'S MEMORY

The encounter at the age of four is an important puzzle piece to this story. It is memories from this age that came flooding back to me after my encounter on the highway. It would take fifteen years from the time of my highway abduction for Janice to completely remember the same memory. It is also what led me full circle, back to my hometown where it all began.

One day while I was visiting my mother in Cranbrook in 1989 Janice came by to visit. The three of us sat talking about what had happened to me, trying to make sense of it all. I asked Janice if she ever remembered anything strange from our childhood. Immediately she said, "I remember there were some strange lights over the shed. You were there, remember?" I did remember and told her so. I asked her what else she remembered and she replied, "Nothing, I just remember seeing the lights over the shed." I knew I couldn't expand on this memory for her, it was important to allow her to remember on her own or she would never believe it was her own memory and not mine.

Months went by after seeing my family. I really wanted to talk to Janice again about that night when we were kids. I was talking to her on the phone when I asked her again about the incident, only giving the details she had supplied. Janice said that I must be mistaken. She didn't remember seeing anything at all and thought I was confused. I didn't push her, understanding that it was a memory that had briefly surfaced, only to go back into her subconscious.

For fourteen years Janice's memory would resurface from time to time. I would start the conversation in the same manner each time, asking her if she ever remembered seeing anything strange. As the years went by she would remember a little more of the incident or forget the whole memory altogether!

(2004)

In 2004 Janice called me from Cranbrook, where she was going to school at the time. She asked me if she could use the incident of us seeing the UFO above the shed for a short story she had to write for a class she was taking. I told her that would be fine with me. She was happy to hear that because she had already written three-quarters of it and wanted to share it with me. After she was done reading it aloud I asked her to verbally tell me the rest of the story. When she finished I said to her, "It's about time you finally got the whole story. Maybe now that you've written it down you won't forget it this time." She asked me what I was talking about. We then talked about what took place that night as children and I told her how she had remembered and forgotten the entire event over the years. I was waiting for her to remember the whole story, *without* my influence. It was amazing, even to me, the detail in which she described that night! She was just as surprised to hear that it was identical in every way to what I remembered. We have the exact same memory.

Later that week, once she finished writing the story she read it to me again. I found it funny that in between the time she verbally told me the end and then finished writing the story she forgot the blue ball of light that sent a beam of light into her head. When she recounted the story the previous week she had remembered this, yet she had quickly reverted to her old trick of forgetting the detail.

After Janice finally remembered this encounter, I decided to tell her about the gift the Aliens had given me. To my astonishment she remembered it. When she told me where it was I was once again given confirmation that the things I was remembering were real! Janice had a clear memory that I had wrapped the gift in a piece of white cloth before putting it in the ground. I said nothing to her about where it was or about the cloth, yet she knew about both. She said I told her she was not allowed to touch it and that we had to make sure our father did not find it! When I asked her what it looked like her memory was very similar to mine. Her description was very close to mine in regards to its shape as well as its size. When we thought about the object it conjured the same visual image and association of another object, a domino.

Janice also said she had a memory of telling our father about the craft and the orb the day after I was taken in 1970. Apparently he laughed and thought it was pretty funny. He said something must have gone wrong because she was not supposed to be there! Strange response for a father whose child had just been taken by Aliens! I have no memory of this reaction from him.

CHANGING MY BLOOD

The memory of my blood being changed when I was four-years old was something the Aliens did not want me to tell people about for a very long time. I'm not clear as to why.

My brother-in-law passed away in April of 2000. A few months later I was still feeling his presence. One Saturday I noticed an advertisement in the paper for a psychic fair. I decided to check it out. Being psychic myself I walked around to see if I got a good vibe off anyone. On my first round I chose a blond-haired woman in her late thirties and on my second round I walked over to her to see if she wanted to give me a reading. This was not something I normally did but on this particular day I felt compelled to do so.

As soon as I walked over to her she had me take a seat to begin the reading. Before I got comfortable she told me someone who recently passed away was standing beside me. I knew my brother-in-law was walking with me that day. She added that she thought it was my brother. I told her she was picking up on my brother-in-law. I knew at that point she was a true psychic.

The woman then used Tarot cards to give me the reading. Nothing of significance was told to me up to that point. She then put the cards away and took both my hands and turned them upward to look at the palms. As she was holding my hands she all of a sudden let go and said, "What was that? I saw doctors all around you when you were a young child. I saw tubes sticking out of your arms. Is there something wrong with your blood?" I knew right away what she was picking up on and I also knew that the Aliens did not want her to see anymore! I tried to change the subject but she took my hands again, this time holding them tighter. "They're changing your blood! Why are they changing your blood? They, they're not doctors—they're Extraterrestrials! Why are they doing that?!" She was shaking and her voice was rattled. Clearly she was shaken by the image and abruptly let go of my hands. "Wow! They don't want me to see that! I asked them what they were doing and they told me it was none of my damn business and to stop looking!"

The woman was shaken by this vision and rather quickly wrapped up the session. I knew the moment she asked me why there were doctors all around me that it was the Aliens she was seeing! I never saw this woman again. The incident she was picking up on was from when I was four-years old. She was clearly seeing the memory I had of the Aliens changing my blood.

The memories of my blood being changed as a child were confirmed to me by a complete stranger. This was one more thing showing me confirmation that all my memories from that experience at age four were real and the complete truth.

CLONES

There are so many aspects to Ufology that it is impossible to address all of them. In my experiences I have found that many of them are so strange on the surface that it's difficult at times for people to believe they're true. One of those experiences has been with the men I called the clones.

When I talk to people about these men I am often left with more questions than answers. I don't know who they are, but what I do know is how they affected my life. The real question is why have they remained in my life for such a long period of time? Why am I of interest to them? I may never know the answers to these questions.

It's been years since I've seen Bill or John. They disappeared in 1991 after I began to question them as to who they were and whom they really worked for. Seth was the last clone to come into my life. He never talked to me about anything out of the ordinary. On the contrary, we spoke of average, mundane things. After I left my job at the café he still showed up in my life every now and then. I would run into him on the street or in a bookstore; occasionally he would come in to my new place of employment. For the next twelve years, every time I booked a flight to go anywhere, I would run into him within one week of booking the flight.

I once told the guy I was dating the whole story about these clones as I reserved a flight to visit my family. I told him that the only time I run into Seth is within one week of my flight bookings; of course my boyfriend didn't believe me. Two days later my boyfriend came by to pick me up from my apartment. He asked me to wait out front so he didn't have to park his car and we could just leave. I went outside to wait and…yes, there was Seth asking me about any new trips I may be going on.

I clearly remember one occasion where I was waiting to run into him, having booked a vacation. I was walking down Granville Street on my way to see a movie. There was still plenty of time before it started so I was walking slowly, looking in the shop windows. As I did so, I noticed Seth in the reflection of the glass. Instead of turning around I walked even slower and stood for a longer time at the next window to see if he would pass me. What he did shocked me! He looked directly at me, stopped, and then turned around as if he was looking at something. This went on for about 8 minutes. It was clear he was waiting for me to notice him as there was no doubt he was following me. Paranoia? I don't think so. It was ridiculously clear to me what was going on: he was following me, waiting for an opportunity to run into me without it appearing to be out of the ordinary.

The last time I saw Seth was in 2003, right after I got back from the trip to Arizona with Carrie. For the first time, I hadn't seen him like I usually did before leaving. Instead we ran into each other two days after my return home. He told me how he had been out of town for a few weeks. I guess that would explain why I never saw him before Carrie and I left. He asked if I had gone on any new trips for vacation. I told him I hadn't. I wanted to see his reaction. He then made a very interesting comment: "Today is a beautiful day, it's so hot—it's almost like being in the desert. Have you every been to the desert Miriam?" He had a strange look on his face after he asked. *Wow,* I thought, *that wasn't subtle!*

I said, "Yes, I've been to Tucson years ago and loved it." He must have known I had just returned from Arizona. Why else would he have made the comment about the desert? He pushed the question by asking if I had been there more recently. He then talked about how hot it was there at this time of year. Maybe he thought I would give in and talk with him about my trip. We ended our conversation and once again I was left questioning who he was and why he was there talking with me.

I called Janice after seeing Seth to tell her about the incident. She thought it was rather interesting that he brought up the desert with me. I vowed to Janice that next time I saw him I would confront him outright. Unfortunately, I never saw him again. The last two times I ran into him I had told him a lie to see how he would react. Perhaps it was because I was no longer being honest with him that he saw no point in continuing contact with me. Maybe he knew the next time I saw him I would be confronting him. Who knows—it's just one more question to add to my list.

The *only* time I remember running into Seth when I hadn't reserved a plane ticket was when I had scheduled surgery for a minor ailment. He said hello and then asked how I was. He then told me he thought I didn't look well and asked about my health. I looked just fine and there was no reason for his comment. Again I left the conversation questioning who he was.

FAMILY CONCERNS

In recent years I have had conversations with my father regarding these Alien contacts. In each conversation I ask him to tell me everything he knows about them. His reactions always confuse me even further. Since the beginning, in every conversation I've had with him over the years, he has told me *not* to get involved with the Aliens. He also told me not to tell anyone about them. "It will destroy your life if you tell anyone about them. They destroyed my life and I don't want that to happen to you. Be careful, I'm telling you to just be careful. If you do what they ask you to do, it could destroy you," he said. These are some of the comments my father made to me in our last conversation in 2006. I told him I knew he was holding back what it is he knows. His reaction to my suspicions was to look at me, smile and not say a word. I think his greatest concern is over the obvious ridicule I will receive over admitting that I've had Alien contact.

My sisters and my mother are all supportive of the path I have been following regarding the Aliens, for the most part. They have encouraged me to write this book but not without their own warnings. They, too, are somewhat concerned as to how this will affect my life and how I will deal with the criticism that will follow the release of my story. Over the years my greatest concern has been over the ridicule my family may have to endure because of my experiences.

Since 1988 my life has changed a great deal. How could it not change after everything I have experienced? My knowledge guides me in almost all my decisions: from who my friends are to whom I will date.

THE ULTIMATE QUESTION

In recounting my experiences over the years I have gone through every emotion possible, including denial, anger and, finally, acceptance. At the beginning of my contacts Aliens were not in mainstream culture—quite the opposite actually. It was difficult to find any information regarding this subject and even harder to find people who had any knowledge of them. At the time of my awakening in 1988 it took nine months before I found a single person that knew about the subject. Looking back, I'm grateful that this subject wasn't in mainstream society and culture as it is today. If I had the same experience today, I would question whether or not my memories were real or imagined. With everything I have seen and experienced I don't question if any of it was real or not: I know it is all the truth. No one will ever convince me otherwise.

Question everything and exclude nothing. That is what I believe. Listen to your morals and your instinct. As long as the message the Aliens give me is of peace and compassion, I will continue to listen and be thankful for them in my life. They are The Caretakers of this world and I am grateful for their presence.

I know that many people will read this and *want* to believe that people like myself are schizophrenics. I assure you this is not the case. Although I have written that I speak to them in my mind and have heard them speak to me, this is in no way on a daily, weekly or even monthly basis. It is on rare occasions I have been blessed enough to hear their voices, such as the example I shared with you with about my experience at the swimming pool in Laughlin, Nevada. Although I can reach them through meditation, this is not the same as them contacting me with their booming voices here in the physical world. It is a real challenge to explain to those who have not had these experiences how we communicate.

There are so many aspects to this phenomenon that it is impossible to explain them all in any one book. Try not to focus any one aspect of this phenomenon since diversity will give you a clearer understanding of what is actually happening in the world today. Your list of questions will never get smaller; rather, it will get longer. As one piece of the puzzle is found, ten more are there waiting to take its place—try not to let this discourage you. Each person seems to hold different answers to the pieces to this great puzzle. Keeping an open mind is one of the keys in finding answers to possibly the biggest question in the history of humankind:

WHO ARE THE ALIENS AND WHO ARE WE?

THE MESSAGES

If I were to tell you the full extent of the messages the Aliens gave me then this would be a book longer than any book known to this world. My intention and task is to help educate the people of this world that Aliens do exist and to prepare the world for the possibility of a global event in which the Aliens will make their presence known to humanity.

WARNINGS OF A POSSIBLE FUTURE

The Aliens gave me warnings of a possible future in which the planet and/or the human race could face destruction. They asked me to share with you what role *they* will play if we are threatened as a species or if there is a threat to the Earth itself. It is a peaceful and positive message.

"One day a star will appear in the sky for all of man to see. Nothing or no one will be able to hide its presence from the world. It will be a sign for the people that the end is near and it is time to prepare."

The Aliens gave me, as well as many others around the world, this same message. What they asked of us is to tell the world, so that in the End Times we might not only survive but also prosper in the coming days. They told of a future in which there will be peace and harmony in the world. They said that in the next world there will be a higher level of spiritual awareness and we will more clearly see the connections between the past, present and future.

WHERE AND WHEN IS THIS TRANSFORMATION TO TAKE PLACE?

We are in the beginning stages of this change. All you have to do is turn on the news, listen to the radio or read a paper to know that the world is a very different place than it was a few years ago. Earth changes are one of the signs that the end is near. Flood, drought, tornados, earthquakes, volcanic eruptions, fires and wars—you name it—the Earth is now showing its dislike for the way we are choosing to live.

These Earth changes cause concern in individual countries over their stability. How will they feed their people? How will they keep all the material wealth they currently have? How will they survive if another country shuts off their supply of products? Whether the issue is oil or food, the issue is the same.

In those countries where food supplies are already low and there is drought and starvation our possible future is already apparent. All we need to do is look at the people who have already begun to kill each other over supplies and food to see how the rest of us will be forced to become unless we make drastic changes today.

We as the human race cannot continue to reproduce and consume the way we have been without destroying ourselves. How much longer can we continue to be consumed by greed and decadence? In one lifetime we have almost stripped the planet of precious resources.

IF THERE IS A CATASTROPHE ON THE PLANET YOU NEED TO BE ABLE TO LOOK AFTER YOURSELF

Let's say for the moment that a large solar flare hits the Earth and it wipes out all electricity. How will you stay warm? What food will you eat when the shelves of the stores run dry? Gas won't be available because the pumps need electrical power to work. No electrical power and the world ceases to function. Where will your clean water come from?

What if there is nuclear war? Do you know how to survive? Do you know what to do in the event of a nuclear bomb? Are you currently living in a safer area?

How will you protect yourself from the certain pandemonium that will take place? Do you know how to build shelter, hunt for food, plant food, collect seeds, find water and stay healthy?

The Aliens want the world to know they are out there, watching. They are always close so that they can protect us *from ourselves*. They explained that if those in power were to set in motion steps that would destroy this planet, they would step in to stop it. This would be one of the ways they would make themselves known to the people of the planet en masse. They will not hesitate in stopping any actions that put the planet at risk. Although they are passive and are not at all violent, they will take violent actions if that is the only option left to protect the planet from irreparable damage.

If there is an event that changes the landscape of the Earth—such as war or meteor impacts—they *may* be there to help. They may make the decision to step in and help the people of this planet if a global event happens that would threaten the ecosystem here on Earth. Do not misinterpret this as them taking care of us. That is not at all the case. They will be here to help preserve the planet and *possibly* some of the inhabitants.

It was made very clear to me that only the strong-willed will survive a global catastrophe. Even though the Aliens will not protect us, they could choose to help some of us. They will supply some people with seeds. These seeds are all we need to sustain our lives and live in harmony with the Earth and live a more simple existence. Please don't misunderstand the message. They are not against the use of technology. They ask that we use it responsibly by not harming the Earth.

WHERE ARE THE SAFE LANDS?

Are you in the right area? It was told to me that in the End Times the Four Corners Area of the United States will be *one* of the Safe Lands. They made it very clear that this is only one place on the planet that will be a safe zone. There is a safe area for every region of Earth. By safe they mean *protected by them.*

In no way does this mean that you should pack up and move to this area now. If you are not one of the people meant to be in these safe zones, the Aliens will remove you. They will only allow those with pure hearts to enter and live in these zones. The people who are meant to inhabit this area will all receive a clear message to gather there when the time is right.

In the Safe Lands the Aliens will be there to *protect* the people from outside forces. They will protect them from any person, organization or group that would cause difficulty or harm to the inhabitants that live within the Safe Lands. They may even walk among us during this time to help guide us through the transition. In the possible futures I was shown by the Aliens I was told that there will be great land masses that will be safe from destruction. However, in these other areas they will not be there to protect you,

you will be left on your own to survive. They may hand out seeds to some people but they will not be there to protect you from outside forces. You will have to defend yourself.

Where are the other Safe Lands? The Aliens told me they were all over the planet. Research and find the people in your area—the original people, the people who hold the light. They will be the indigenous people of your area. These people will be highly *spiritual,* having strong beliefs in other worlds, holding all life sacred, and having ancient rituals and ceremonies to uphold those beliefs. They will have been living *peacefully* in the same area for thousands of years, respectful of the Earth and of all life upon it. The ancient people all over the planet that have held the land and held ancient beliefs for thousands of years are the Keepers of the Safe Lands. They will be the Keepers of Knowledge in your area. They are the Shamans and Spiritual leaders of humanity. Find the original inhabitants of your area. There you will find the Safe Land, the land that will be protected by the Aliens in the End Times.

These areas are not centered around organized religions in your area. Although religions do have their place in the world in helping people to understand God, they are not the Keepers of Knowledge that I speak of. This knowledge is an understanding of Earth and of the relationship between a drop of rain, a blade of grass and the Universe itself. Organized religions attempt to teach these concepts but they allow for too many man made ideas and ideals that take away from that understanding.

DO NOT FOLLOW ANY ONE PERSON'S BELIEFS

Do not be fooled by false Keepers of the Knowledge and the Light. There are many who claim to be these people but they are false Prophets. Only those who have not faltered in their beliefs are the true Prophets of the people—those people who have fought to keep their tradition alive and have *succeeded in doing so.*

There are many peoples all over the planet who have lost their belief, their light, and are struggling to get it back. Sadly, these people have forgotten the reason for their beliefs: to be the leaders of the people on the planet and leaders in the End Times. Although they struggle to bring back their knowledge, to restore what they once understood, it may be a task that is no longer possible. The knowledge they once had as the Prophets, the Teachers of the Earth, has diminished. However, they can restore the knowledge of their faith in daily life and, by doing so, live in the New World in peace and harmony.

There are more than a few people who have made the decision to *claim* they are Prophets. Those that make these claims are false Prophets. A true Prophet would make no such claim; they would only follow the word of God and no more. Remember, God asks us to be humble, and claiming the power of prophecy as a person is nothing more than vanity. The truth can be seen by anyone who chooses to look. It does not need to be expressed in personal acclaim. Question everything, and everyone—especially those whose vanity can be seen with your eyes as well as felt with your heart.

There are people in the UFO community who have made claims of being the messengers of the Aliens and have claimed the title of Prophets. It is my understanding from the Aliens themselves that these claims would not be condoned. The reason I say this is because they have expressed to me the importance of never following any one person or any one idea as being the only one. That includes me, and my messages. I ask that you question everything I have told you. *They* ask that you question everything and exclude nothing as the being the ultimate truth. It is only through this process you will find truthful answers.

WHY DO THE ALIENS CARE? WHERE ARE THEY FROM?

Why do the Aliens care and who are they to the people of this planet? I was told that there are some Aliens that are in a physical form living here in underground bases. There are others that live among us, undetected because they look so much like us. There are many others that exist on other dimensions that often are in contact with the people of this planet. Those that are in the other dimensions have a great responsibility to the people here. I was told that they come to us in dreams to help teach us, guide us and talk with us. They are the ones that help raise the consciousness of the world through the dream state. They help to maintain the dream world as well as this world. Both the physical and dimensional beings are in contact with one another and are related, but they are in fact different beings.

The Tall Blonds are here to help protect the planet from outside forces that may not be known to us at this time. They are also here to monitor the planet. Their main directive is to help maintain the planet and the people living on it. They will not allow it to be completely destroyed by us or any other means.

Some of these physical beings live on other planets in the Universe, great distances from us. They are able to travel to Earth but it is a long journey. I was told that some of the Tall Blonds are here now and others are on their way to us. I was given no further information about how they travel or of their world.

It is my understanding that the Tall Blonds have always been a part of Earth and that they helped to seed the Earth with life. Again I ask that you not misinterpret their words. They do not claim to be God. They do have a superior understanding of life itself and of God, but I was told that this understanding was beyond *my* comprehension and unexplainable, so they told me nothing further. They told me that they too search to know God and that they have always been The Caretakers of *worlds*. This is their reason for their existence as well as to learn and grow spiritually as we do here except on different levels of understanding.

The Earth is a very special place because it is unlike any place or other dimensions, other planets or in the Universe. Here we are given a gift of beauty in the form of being separated from everything that surrounds us. Instead of being in light bodies we are dense and heavy here on Earth. We can enjoy the singularity of almost every molecule around us. For this reason we are able to sit quietly and stare at a flower petal or an ant. We can watch and learn from it if that is what we choose to do. We can see into the entire Universe and become closer to God by looking closely at anything in nature, but only if we stop and open our eyes.

In the other worlds/dimensions everything is more intertwined— through telepathy for example. There is a greater understanding of knowledge of other places of existence. Here we have the *gift* of separation and the unknown. The irony is this is often what people have the most difficulty dealing with in life—feeling alone and not knowing what is going to happen in their lives. Once you realize and understand this is the *gift of life*, you can then begin to live with gratitude in your heart for everything you experience. Take time each day to see the beauty of the world, no matter how difficult your life is. When you glimpse the true beauty in nature you can feel the love of God touch your soul.

One of the reasons we are important to the Aliens is because everything we do affects the other worlds and dimensions. All other planes of existence are interconnected with ours. Simply because we are still too ignorant to be able to see how this is fact does not make it false. If we destroy the *planet* then we ultimately change the very existence of all that is. If we harm the planet and ourselves as a species, then we are harming God. God is the true creator of all that is, all that was and all that will be. What is lost will never be again as the whole plan of life itself is changed because of it. I cannot explain this further in a way that would make any sense. This is what was told to me by the Aliens and, in some way, the understanding of this was placed within me.

HOW HUMAN KIND WAS CREATED AND WHO THE HOPI ARE

When I sat in a chair onboard the craft that day in 1988, I was shown the creation of man on a screen and told how we came to be. The Tall Blond Aliens had a hand in the creation of this planet and all the life upon it. They are The Caretakers of this world and made it clear to me that they are not our God.

THERE WERE THREE WORLDS PRIOR TO THIS ONE

In the first world the Aliens took the seeds of human life and of all animal life and spread them out across the world. They were patient and watched as humankind was being formed. Sadly, after a great deal of time, the life that sprang forward was unaware and simple. It became apparent that this first world was not going to evolve much further than it had. With great sadness the world was cleaned of all of the life that had not evolved and the Aliens began to seed the second world.

In the second world it was decided that more form was to be given to the life on the planet and once again the seed of all life forms was created and placed all over the earth. The shells of the life forms were created so they could focus less on physical growth and more on conscious growth and awareness. A great deal of time was given to this life in the hope that it would grow into conscious beings and begin the process of spiritual growth. The process of waiting for life to become self-aware turned out to be pointless.

The life that formed did not evolve at all towards its own awareness, let alone learn anything of spiritual growth and understanding. The animals that roamed the Earth grew into nothing more than killing machines with basic survival skills. They fought with each other and again it was decided to remove all the life forms that had not evolved past the initial seeding stage. For this reason it was decided to give humankind what it needed physically in the new world so that spiritual growth would be its focus.

Humankind's reason for being would be to give all conscious life in the rest of creation a place where they could enjoy the different aspects of life. People could do this because, as humans, they were able to be in an altered state of consciousness of singularity rather than being part of the oneness of all things. Knowledge of the Universe and spiritual understanding was made into the fabric of humankind.

This process took a long time. It was through careful consideration that it was decided animal life would be allowed to have a basic awareness of itself in the third world. Even more thought was given to the creation of human beings. The Aliens' intent was to help each individual soul evolve spiritually over time so that all life from outside the Earth could visit this planet using the human body as their vehicle.

This third world began as an almost Utopian society. It was a beautiful planet and the experience of man and woman living upon it gave the individual soul that visited a great deal of insight into everything in a way that had never been experienced before. It was a success until the lives of many humans began to be taken for granted. These people had great knowledge of what was outside of their bodies, understanding that the shell they lived in was only temporary and that life would go on after they left the planet in death. Unfortunately, these people lacked maturity in emotional and spiritual growth.

It was when humans began to change the creation of themselves and animals that the third world began to fall apart. Not content to live in harmony on the Earth, some of the beings that came to Earth in the physical form decided it was time to begin changing the look and function of the human body. The result was disastrous. It brought with it awful experiments that were done without hesitation: rather quickly dictatorship and discontent descended upon the planet. As the third world turned from peaceful to violent, perfect to grotesque, the decision was made to cleanse the Earth of the destructive force that had taken hold. Lack of spiritual maturity, too much knowledge without responsibility and negative forces caused the world to turn to chaos.

Although the purpose of humankind was to allow free will and spiritual growth for the individual soul, it was clear that by giving it all the understanding of the Universe it became ungrateful for the gift of living on Earth. People thought that because they could not be destroyed they could then do as they pleased and create whatever they wanted without thought. These were dark and evil forces at work on the planet.

The planet was to be cleansed of this ungrateful evil. It was decided to take back some of the knowledge that was given in the third world so that people could slowly grow to understand that knowledge and be more mature and responsible with it. They began again with a new human. While making this decision it became clear that there were pockets of people all over the planet that had done exactly what the Creator had intended: they lived in harmony with the Earth. They were the spiritual leaders of the planet and lived a peaceful existence in which they understood the past, present and future. They did no harm to anyone or anything and abided by Universal laws of gratitude.

It was decided that these people—the pure of heart—could be taken from the third world and brought into the fourth. They would be taken from the planet by the Aliens and given safe harbour until the world was cleansed once again and it was time for them to live on the Earth, this time in the fourth world.

When I was shown the third world I saw a group of spiritual people living on the planet at that time. They were the seers and the Keepers of Knowledge. I was told that these were the only people who were taken from the third world into the fourth. When they were brought to this world they were told that they were to keep the knowledge of the prior worlds and the spiritual knowledge they had. They were to hold the knowledge until the End Times of this, the fourth world. They were to maintain the knowledge of these things and teach all those that came after them to this world so that what happened in the last world would not happen again. They were told that they would be called upon in this fourth world to gather the people in the End Times so that they could once again be taken from this world and brought into the next world. I was told that one day I would find these people and they would be the ones to gather the chosen. Some of those that are gathered will stay here on Earth in the Safe Lands, while others will be taken to live with the Aliens. These people will be given safe harbour in the Alien world until the New World, the *fifth world,* is safe for them to return to.

When I saw the Hopi men that day at Keams Canyon and saw the spirals in their eyes, I recognized them as being these special people who were taken from the last world and brought into this, the fourth world. I knew in that exact moment who they were. They were the Keepers of the Knowledge of the last world and had been told the promises of the next world. I knew they were important to many people all over the world. They had the power to stand together and influence the people of this planet. They had been given this task and accepted this responsibility when they entered this world. It is for this reason they hold their ceremonies—it is for us—for the past, the present and the future of humanity itself. It is for the Earth and all that lay upon it. They accepted that responsibility for the preservation of this entire Universe, to hold the center of all that is. *They*—the Hopi—are the past, present and future of humankind.

The Hopi people have relatives all over the planet and they are not alone. They were separated when they entered the fourth world and placed all over the Earth. All these people are the Keepers of the Knowledge. When these people are brought back together, then and only then will the world listen. The Keepers came from the spiritual centers around the third world. Some that came to this world brought with them more knowledge than others, while some were taught more than others by the Aliens. The Native American Hopi people are from the highest spiritual level in the last world. It is for this reason they have been able to hold this knowledge for such a long time in this world. They are strong and powerful people, with the ability to remember who they are and where they are going without allowing anything to stand in the way of their beliefs and tradition. They understand the importance of the job they were given: to teach the people of Earth to live in harmony with all things. They are also to lead the people in the End Times from the fourth world into the fifth.

If they fail in this task of holding the knowledge until the Aliens return, they will not be taken from this world into the next. If they fail, they will fail at gathering the chosen. Humankind would cease to exist as we know it today and all of humanity could be wiped clean from the planet only to start over again. It is time for people to stop and not only listen to the true Keepers of Knowledge on the planet, but also to act on their wisdom. If we follow their words of wisdom, we will all live in great peace, contentment and harmony in the New World.

CLOSING COMMENTS

As I stated at the beginning of this chapter, I could write a book longer than any known on Earth and still I could not tell you all the information the Aliens gave to me.

Acknowledging we are not alone is the first step. Once you *accept* that we are not alone the next step is to act upon that fact. Respect your life and the lives of all living things. Walk through this life with respect for the Earth. If you can do this then you can no longer harm yourself, others, the Earth or the other dimensions and worlds. *You* are the creation of God. Act responsibly with that knowledge.

The final message is simple: we are not alone. Listen to the wisdom of the Ancient Civilizations and the Aliens, both are here to help guide us to a new way of life. There is a divine plan; the Alien presence is a safeguard to protect everything that was created by God. There is no reason to fear them when they arrive.

Watch the skies for the Blue Star to appear.

UTOPIA

I close my eyes and there before me
I see the Universe
from a single creature to every living thing
the vibrant colours
filled with anticipation of being truly discovered
walking along a golden path of light leading to Utopia
a world of colour and emotion of few words spoken
it is of beginnings with no real endings
a Shangri-La of the worlds combined as one
the Universe lay before you
in a single breath you inhale the tranquility
of this other world
without a name of an unknown place
in your mind it is as real as yourself
without your presence it disappears once again
out there in the unknown
until the next one stumbles across this haven
the closed eyes of the mystical wanderer
sees more of life than the man
that walks the street with eyes wide open
he sees no more than land and people
from where he asks
they are from Utopia the unknown land
where souls were born
of life ever lasting and ever beginnings
a place called Shangri-La
a simple traveler can reach this place
if only he finds the golden path of light
and follows it without fear but with love in his heart
a direction that few are willing to circum to
the beauty of ones self
to reach high enough
and enter into the unknown…

Made in United States
Troutdale, OR
06/21/2024

20722602R00123